ASSET MANAGEMENT IN
THEORY AND PRACTICE

Asset
management
In Theory and Practice

Duncan Hughes

Financial World Publishing
IFS House
4-9 Burgate Lane
Canterbury
Kent
CT1 2XJ
United Kingdom

T   01227 812012
F   01227 479641
E   editorial@ifslearning.com
W   www.ifslearning.com

Financial World Publishing publications are published by The Chartered Institute of Bankers, a non-profit making registered educational charity.

The Chartered Institute of Bankers believes that the sources of information upon which the book is based are reliable and has made every effort to ensure the complete accuracy of the text. However, neither CIB, the author nor any contributor can accept any legal responsibility whatsoever for consequences that may arise from errors or omissions or any opinion or advice given.

Trademarks

Many words in this publication in which the author and publisher believe trademarks or other proprietary rights may exist have been designated as such by use of Initial Capital Letters. However, in so designating or failing to designate such words, neither the author nor the publisher intends to express any judgement on the validity or legal status of any proprietary right that may be claimed in the words.

Typeset by Kevin O'Connor
Printed by
© Chartered Institute of Bankers 2002
ISBN 0-85297-620-8

CONTENTS

CHAPTER 1

Introduction

Purpose

The aim of this book is to introduce the reader to the asset management industry and to provide an insight into the real-life environment in which fund managers work. Much has been written regarding investment theory: the benefits of diversifying a portfolio of assets, managing its risk, immunizing fixed interest portfolios against interest rate changes, etc. This book endeavours to relate this theory to the practices of asset management firms and the multitude of complex constraints under which they work.

The scope of this book is shown in the following context diagram; functions outside of the dotted boundary are not covered in any detail.

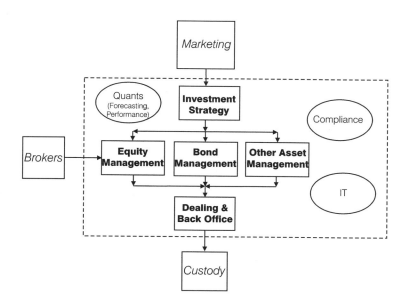

The core of the book centres on the main investment decision-making process highlighted in bold function squares within the dotted context boundary.

Structure

As stated above, the main purpose of this book is to give the reader a 'big picture' view of the workings of, and the challenges facing, the modern asset management industry from an investment (rather than from, for example, a marketing) perspective. In exploring these challenges, formulae and numerical examples are provided wherever possible to bring to life textual descriptions. It is important, however, that the reader does not get 'bogged down' with any maths, instead moving on to the next chapter before returning to specific subjects of interest for more detailed study.

Where relevant, therefore, chapters introduce their subject from a theoretical standpoint before discussing the impact of constraints facing asset managers. Simplified examples are used to illustrate key points, ie the 'building blocks', before moving on to more complex models.

The appendices provided are by no means filled with irrelevant 'padding' but contain, albeit at a high level, overviews of important concepts and events with serious implications for asset managers. The reason for their segregation in appendices is to maintain the momentum of the flow of developing ideas.

What Is Asset Management?

The role of asset managers is to obtain for their customers a superior return on their capital, through investing this capital in global securities markets on their clients' behalf. 'Superior return' means adding value in the following ways:

- Making better investment decisions than their clients could, due to their research capacity and investment skill

- Providing a level of investment diversification through the pooling of funds that their clients could not achieve

- Using their breadth of knowledge and experience to fulfil the investment objectives of the fund, eg providing an acceptable pension for their client

The return on investment is compared to a benchmark, often constructed from the returns obtained by rival asset managers, this comparison being used by investors to assess the asset manager's performance. The asset manager is also responsible for ensuring that the client's individual preferences and needs are observed, eg level of risk appetite, liquidity needs, tax implications etc. Asset managers usually look after more than one client, each client's capital being segregated into a 'fund' or 'portfolio'[1]. Asset management is also referred to variously as 'investment management', 'fund management' and 'portfolio management'. The management of high net worth individuals' assets is usually carried out by specialist private client departments, who face the challenge of managing a very large number of clients, especially when compared to pension fund managers. Investment management is not to be confused with 'investment banking', which is a very different business, focusing much more on corporate clients and their financing needs (such as restructuring a corporation's debt or equity).

A key element in the asset management industry is regulation. In order for investors to have confidence in placing their capital with asset managers, it is essential that they view the industry as being properly regulated. Although for UK asset managers the requirements for regulatory compliance are onerous, the success of the UK asset management industry in particular is due, *inter alia*, to the existence of a credible and effective regulatory system.

The types of fund management offered by asset managers are analogous to products in other industries. Asset managers are compared to their peers, with performance comparisons being frequently reported in the press, enabling the investing public make an informed decision with regard to their choice of asset manager.

There are really very few important differences between products, these differences emanating from the purpose of the fund (which in turn dictates which securities it can invest in), and the regulatory and tax rules with

---

[1] Pension, life and insurance capital (also known as 'institutional investment') is usually referred to as a 'fund', whereas private individuals' wealth is usually referred to as a 'portfolio'.

which the fund manager must comply. Types of products include the following:

Segregated Funds

A segregated fund is a group of assets belonging to one particular client. In addition to holding securities such as equities, bonds and cash directly, it may also hold units of other funds. This 'fund of funds' structure will be covered in more detail later.

Pension Fund Management

The key differential between pension funds and other types of funds is the tax advantage allowed to these fund types, with the proviso that investors are restricted from enjoying the benefits of their savings until they reach a qualifying retirement age.

Pension fund management is very carefully supervised, both by government appointed regulators and by the guardians of the fund, the Trustees. This is due to the important nature of these funds, ie that they exist to provide pensioners with their income to support them in retirement. As an example, Trustees are very often reluctant to allow pension funds to invest in derivatives, due to the high risk reputation that these instruments have (rather unjustly) gained in recent years.

An important factor in pension fund management is the 'age' of the pension fund, this being based on the average age of investors who are investing in the fund. This is important, since for 'young' pension funds the main objective will be to maximize long term growth through a high weighting in equities which have, historically, consistently outperformed other classes of assets in the long run. As the pension fund ages, higher weightings are generally allocated to bonds and cash in order that the risk of a sharp (if temporary) drop in equity markets when pensioners require their funds is minimized. Bonds and cash will also give the fund the liquidity required to pay investors' pension entitlements (these are usually converted from a lump sum received from the pension fund into an annuity to provide the investor with a regular income).

The flow of cash payments representing the payment of pension lump sums is referred to as the fund's 'liability stream', the implications of which will be covered in more detail later. Some pension schemes, such as company pensions, offer a guaranteed income (for example based on the employee's salary at retirement). Many, however, provide no guarantees as to the level of pension that will be provided, simply paying the investor his 'share' at retirement age. It is left to the Trustees to monitor the performance of the fund, with the ultimate sanction of moving the capital to another asset manager if they feel that the incumbent fund manager is consistently underperforming. The existence of this sanction, when combined with the fierce competition for pension fund mandates, puts a great deal of pressure on fund managers to deliver returns superior to those achieved by their rivals.

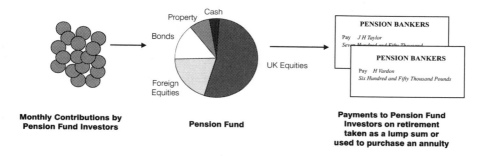

Monthly Contributions by Pension Fund Investors   **Pension Fund**   **Payments to Pension Fund Investors on retirement taken as a lump sum or used to purchase an annuity**

Life Fund Management

Life funds are long term investment plans designed to provide the owner with a lump sum at the end of a relatively long investment horizon (typically in excess of 15 years). These products are usually 'bundled' with life insurance (hence the name) and have traditionally been a poor short-term investment when customers have tried to cash the policies in the early years of the policy. This is because sales commission was taken out of the initial payments, leaving the investor with very little invested in the fund in the early years. Owing to the number of complaints received by regulators, asset management companies' representatives (usually Independent Financial Advisors (IFAs) or the companies' own direct sales force) are now obliged to explain the pros and cons of each product fully. They are also required to give each customer a 'cooling off' period during which they can change their mind regarding any products to which they may have subscribed.

Endowment Policies

Endowment policies are designed to pay off a client's mortgage after a specified number of years. Most make no actual commitment to actually pay the amount required. Rather, they state that based on an assumed annual return the capital invested will be sufficient to cover the required amount. The fund manager's objective will be to achieve the rate of return required to provide the investor with enough capital to repay the mortgage while taking the lowest possible risk.

Insurance Fund Management

Insurance funds represent the pooling of insurance companies' customers' premiums, and are held in a fund in order to meet claims arising out of policies issued by the insurance company. The fund manager is generally required to ensure that adequate cash can be made available when required to meet claims. In some instances fund managers are required to match the anticipated cash flows from claims (the liability stream) with cash flows from the fund. The stream of cash flows can come from bond coupons and redemptions and equity dividends, in addition to the sale of securities to meet cash requirements. As with most fund types, a proportion of the fund will be held in cash to meet any immediate requirements; however, this will drag the fund's performance down in a time of rising equity markets.

Private Client Portfolios

Private client portfolios represent the invested wealth of high net worth individuals. Private client fund managers are required to balance the client's requirement for long term growth with requirements for an income stream and liquidity to meet immediate cash requirements.

Hedge Funds

Hedge funds are basically funds which are leveraged, ie their exposure to global markets exceeds the capital invested in the fund [2]. There are two main methods of achieving this leverage. The most obvious way is to use derivatives; the fund only needs to cover derivative exchanges' margin requirements, and can therefore build very large positions using a limited amount of capital. Another method is through selling short securities that the fund manager predicts will fall in value. The cash from the sale of these

[2] For an explanation of the concept of leverage, please refer to Appendix I.

6

securities not held by the fund manager is then used to purchase securities which the fund manager predicts will rise in value, thereby enormously reducing the overall capital requirement of the fund. The back office implications of selling securities that you do not own are covered in Chapter 10.

Index Tracking Funds

These funds differ from all other types of funds in that they are 'passively' as opposed to 'actively' managed. The idea here is that, since equity markets have been observed to outperform other asset categories in the long term, the fund manager will set up and run a fund that mimics the index. Many indices have far more securities than a fund manager could comfortably cope with in a fund (eg the Standard and Poor's 500 index). The skill therefore lies in minimizing the 'tracking error' (ie the variance of the difference in returns between the fund and the index it is replicating) with a reasonable number of holdings (say a maximum of 100). These funds have been very successful in recent years, mainly because of a good performance record when compared to active managers. Additionally, lower management fees are charged for this type of fund, making it an attractive option.

Unitized Vehicles

These products are marketed to the public to enable investors to gain exposure to global securities markets via funds holding underlying securities in one or more markets. Investors can buy units of these funds whenever they wish to (rather than being committed to regular monthly payments as they would be for most pension and life plans); they can also easily sell their units at the prevailing market rate to realize a profit, or to raise cash. Essentially small investors are pooling their capital to enable them to invest in a relatively large number of diversified companies, which they would not easily be able to do due to the cost of holding very small quantities of shares. According to modern portfolio theory, these diversified investment products represent a 'superior' option to direct investment in individual companies and should, therefore, represent an attractive option to private investors.

These funds are also used by segregated fund managers to gain exposure to different markets. For example, a pension fund manager might hold units of several 'investing' unitized vehicles, rather than investing directly in securities themselves.

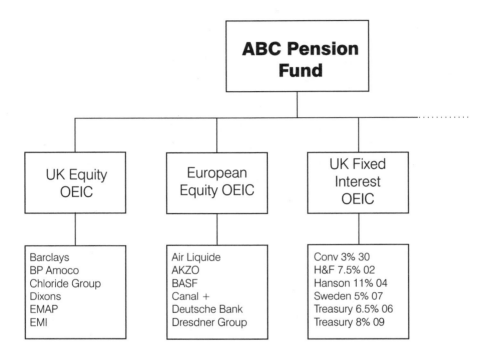

There are significant benefits to fund managers in adopting this 'fund of funds' approach, since it enables pension fund managers, working with market strategists, to concentrate on the global big picture, while market specialists can focus on stock selection within their particular market.

Unit Trusts

These funds are trusts created to manage securities on behalf of a relatively large number of small investors. The fund is divided into units which are bought and sold by investors at the prevailing market rate, this being very closely related to the market value of the underlying securities in which the unit trust invests. Trading in units must be carried out through the fund manager (ie there is no secondary market). The number of units is variable, ie the amount of capital invested in the fund can change, such changes being known as unit creation for an increase in capital, and liquidation for a decrease. An important back office function is the administration of the buying, selling, creation and liquidation of units, in addition to the accurate pricing of the fund once or more per day, this being a regulatory requirement. Unit trusts are referred to as 'mutual funds' in the United States.

Investment Trusts

Investment trusts are companies formed for the specific purpose of investing in securities, having a fixed amount of capital (which under regulatory rules cannot change). They differ from unit trusts in that investors buy shares in this Investment Trust Company (ITC), rather than units of a unit trust fund. Since it is a company, the ITC can borrow additional money to invest, resulting in an overall geared (or leveraged) position. ITCs are also able to hedge any currency risks. Unlike unit trusts, ITC share values do not always reflect the value of the underlying assets, often being quoted at a discount to reflect borrowed funds and additional risk.

Open Ended Investment Companies (OEICs)

OEICs are a recent innovation which vary very little from ITCs apart from their ability to vary their capital. As investors buy shares, the number of shares increases (ITCs, with their fixed capital, would experience a rise in their share price's value). Due to the comparative ease of administration many unit trusts have been converted to OEICs.

The Global Asset Management Industry

Nearly all of the world's wealth is held in the form of recognizable funds (or portfolios). In essence, these funds are nothing more than a group of assets such as equities, bonds, property and cash held in proportions which, the fund manager believes, will meet the his clients' objectives. A very large proportion of the world's capital is now held in the form of pension, unitized (known as 'mutual' in the US) and insurance funds. This is a symptom of a fundamental and on-going redistribution of wealth from a very small minority to the wage-earning and pension-drawing majority. This shift has created the requirement for specialist fund managers to invest on behalf of fund owners, with the specific objective of maximizing the owners' long term wealth, ie investing their capital in assets offering the highest return for an acceptable level of risk.

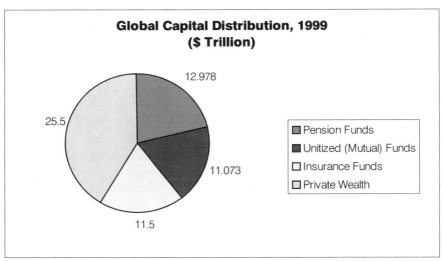

Global Capital Distribution, 1999 ($ Trillion)

12.978

25.5

11.073

11.5

- ▨ Pension Funds
- ▩ Unitized (Mutual) Funds
- ☐ Insurance Funds
- ☐ Private Wealth

Source: Merrill Lynch, CCF Charterhouse

The growth of the global asset management industry is set to continue as continental Europe continues to catch up with the levels of pension fund provisioning observed in the US, Japan and the UK. In addition, the increasing propensity of global fund managers to invest in international equities is resulting in expansion of asset management companies to establish a local presence in the markets in which they invest.

The Difficulty of Professional Investment

Fund managers live in a very challenging environment. This is not least because they are generally torn between their own analysis (ie whether, based on their research, they 'like' a stock), and the reality that just as important is what the consensus of the investment community *will be*. This is because, however well a fund manager chooses stocks that deserve capital to be allocated to them, he will only benefit (ie gain a performance advantage) if the investment community falls into line with his thinking. The fact that everyone is playing this game (ie trying to second guess the future consensus view) only makes the market more complex. Related to this point is that the market generally prices its expectations in ahead of actual news being released. Thus when news is released, its impact will be observed in terms of deviations from the previous expectation, not from the actual observed news. This naturally makes market analysis very difficult to unpick.

CHAPTER 2

Asset Management House Organizational Structure

All asset management houses have different organizational structures. The purpose of this chapter is to describe the roles performed by a typical asset management house's directors and staff, paying particular attention to the roles most closely affecting the core business of managing clients' assets.

Management

A sample organization chart is provided overleaf. Actual management structures of asset management companies are rarely this straightforward; many UK companies are owned by European or American parents making reporting lines less clear. However, the broad responsibilities and chief current challenges of senior directors are generally as follows.

Chief Executive Officer	Responsible for the overall management and direction of the company, particularly in terms of building an effective and cohesive team to manage the business
Chief Investment Officer	Takes responsibility for the delivery of fund performance and, in particular, endeavours to consistently outperform the company's rivals. In most modern fund management companies it is the CIO's responsibility to promote a team approach (rather than a 'star fund manager' culture)
Chief Financial Officer	Essentially the finance director, but also usually responsible for general administration

Chief Operating Officer	Overseer of the company's operations, particularly in the area of ensuring that transactions carried out on behalf of clients are properly processed. Importantly must ensure that the systems are in place to ensure compliance with regulations, and that all client and regulatory reporting is carried out to the satisfaction of trustees and regulators
IT Director	This role is becoming increasingly important as more and more reliance is placed on, *inter alia*, the electronic sourcing of market and other data, the automation of asset management processes (eg the drive toward STP[3]), and the electronic marketing of products over the Internet (particularly unitized vehicles)
Marketing Director	This function is absolutely essential to modern day asset management. The asset management company needs to sell itself to all of the different segments of the market, pension funds, life funds and 'retail' (generally unitized vehicles sold via Independent Financial Advisers (IFAs)). There is an increasing trend in the use of e-commerce to market asset management products, particularly unitized vehicles, as markets open up across Europe.
Strategy Director	Has asset allocation responsibility, ie makes the highest level decisions with regard to allocation of funds between equities, bonds, property and cash. May also make decisions regarding allocation between equity markets. Usually responsible for ensuring strategy implementation in a timely and consistent fashion. Economists in his team will analyse fundamental data and trends to forecast future market conditions.
Compliance Officer	Responsible for ensuring that the asset management firm operates within the parameters required by regulators such as the FSA and clients

[3] STP is 'Straight Through Processing' where asset management seek to maximize opportunities to automate such processes as Broker Confirmation and Settlement (which are covered in detail in Chapter 10).

Back Office	Provides administrative services such as settlement for transactions carried out with brokers, reconciliation with the client's custodians and maintenance of records of unitized fund transactions
Quants	Provide performance, risk and other analyses for both internal feedback and client reporting

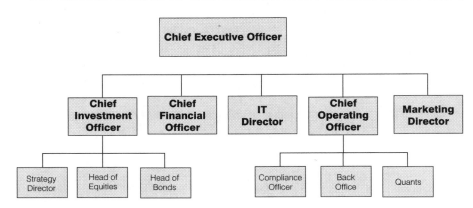

Fund Management

The fund manager takes overall responsibility for the fund from an investment perspective, ie its performance, risk profile and dealing on the client's behalf. Day to day contact (eg to provide valuations of portfolios and other information) is generally carried out by a separate client services team. Fund managers are responsible for 'beating' (ie achieving a higher return than) their benchmark (eg the Morgan Stanley Capital International World Equity index, J P Morgan, Salomon Brothers etc). The fund manager will also often be responsible for ensuring that the fund has cash available when required to meet obligations (usually called the liability stream) of the fund (eg to pay pension entitlements, insurance claims etc).

Fund management responsibility is usually carried out by senior investment staff with other, often related, roles. Generally the larger the client, the more senior the fund manager (who may also be known as the Investment Director); thus the CIO may take on the investment director's role for a large pension fund mandate, whereas a UK equity desk Energy specialist might also take on fund management responsibility for a UK Equity OEIC.

House policy on markets and stocks is reviewed at each investment department's (or 'desk's') morning meeting. This meeting is used to share information with regard to economic and market conditions, as well as trading and other activities planned for the day.

In addition to their role as market and security analysts, fund managers also take responsibility for ensuring that orders are executed accurately, ie that the correct line of stock has been ordered, that sufficient cash will be available for settlement and sold stock is available for delivery (by checking with the custodian responsible for stock certificates). Fund managers are also responsible for ensuring that all clients receive equal treatment, ie stocks are to be bought simultaneously across all similar funds.

Equity Management

The global equity market is generally divided into regions of the world, each region having a dedicated 'desk' and with specialization occurring in emerging markets. For example, French and German markets would be handled by the mainstream European desk, whereas Eastern European markets might be separately handled by an Emerging European specialist.

Each desk's resources are roughly determined by the value of the funds for which they are responsible. For most UK based fund managers, the UK Equity desk is usually the largest given the (unexplained by modern portfolio theory) large allocations made to the domestic market. UK equity desks can usually afford, in terms of resources, to have industry specialists (eg Finance, Consumer Goods etc), whereas overseas desks, eg the European Desk, may have country specialists.

Security research involves collating data from the vast quantity of broker research provided, preparing house earnings estimates and modelling the impact of changes on earnings forecasts of economic news and changes in market consensus (eg interest rate changes, oil price changes etc).

Fixed Interest Management

In addition to beating his benchmark, the fixed interest fund manager will also often be responsible for ensuring that the fund has cash available when required to meet obligations (usually called the liability stream) of the fund (eg to pay pension entitlements, projected insurance claims etc).

Fixed interest market research primarily involves the analysis of factors affecting the prices of bonds. Interest rate changes have the most dramatic and sweeping effects, but for individual bonds changes to credit ratings (ie if the risk of default changes) can also have a dramatic effect. Research and analysis centres on the forecasting of factors which may affect interest rates (eg wage inflation, Federal Reserve Board (FRB) policy statements) and credit rating changes (eg poor company results, notification from Moody's or S&P of a change in rating, or being put on creditwatch). Administrative duties include coupon washing (selling and then buying back securities to avoid the liability to pay tax on coupons) and reinvestment of cash (eg upon maturity of a bond).

Property Management

Property management is a very specialized area, and is often carried out by property fund managers working in a separate company within an asset management group. Investment is focused mainly on commercial property. Issues surrounding property management include price levels and rental income levels. Administration of leases and rent payments represents a significant overhead in this business area.

Other key differences between this area and other security markets include high transaction overheads (lawyers' fees, processing paperwork etc) and the indivisibility of large holdings. Very inelastic supply (generally due to the fact that there is finite land space and it is difficult to knock buildings down or gain permission to build on preserved land to change supply) is another key factor in the property market. In addition, repairs and maintenance costs need to be factored into the cost of ownership. Regulation is severe, especially concerning tenants' rights. Accurate valuation is difficult without actually selling a property, due to a lack of comparable properties and long rent agreements.

Cash Management

The objective of cash managers (also known as the 'Treasury Desk') is to achieve the maximum return for capital formally allocated by a fund manager to the Cash security class. They are also responsible for the management of cash which is required for settlement in a number of days, but is available for investment now. Their role is to 'sweep' cash into Treasury Bills, Call Deposits, Short Term Income Funds (STIFs) or other money market instruments offering attractive interest rates. Specifically, they are responsible for ensuring that the fund does not go overdrawn and that cash does not remain uninvested overnight.

Dealers

The role of a dealer in an asset management house is quite different from the role of a dealer in an investment bank or market making operation. Rather than having his own 'book', ie trading on his own account to make a profit (or loss), an asset management dealer is responsible for buying or selling securities on behalf of the asset management house's clients at the most favourable price available at the time of dealing. Dealers will obtain prices for securities from a number of brokers and select the best price available at that time for the lot that they are trading (this is usually a 'bulk' deal on behalf of a number of the asset manager's clients at a time). Dealers are also responsible for agreeing the terms of trades with the broker after the trade (eg accrued interest to be paid on bond deals), including any custodial delivery arrangements.

Stock Lending

A valuable source of income can be obtained by lending securities owned by funds to other financial institutions who need to deliver a security that they do not own. This need can arise through errors being made when selling out of a position, or by speculators in the market deliberately selling short a security that they do not own in the hope that the value of the security will fall, thereby generating a profit.

Quantitative Analysis

The Quants desk is responsible for providing asset managers with essential data relating to the fund. This includes fund returns (ie how the fund has performed) and performance attribution (ie why it has performed as it has). These figures are produced for both internal and external consumption. This department is also generally responsible for providing risk measures and exposure reporting.

Marketing

In today's competitive marketplace, an asset manager's marketing function is absolutely vital. The role of this department encompasses direct selling (both to institutional investors such as pension funds as well as individuals looking to invest in unitized vehicles), communicating the company's investment approach and product range to intermediaries such as Independent Financial Advisers (IFAs) and the account management of existing clients.

Back Office

The Back Office, as it is collectively referred, actually performs a number of key functions, many of which are required by regulatory bodies to be carried out on an accurate and timely basis. The functions include settlement of trades carried out by dealers, handling of corporate actions occurring on existing holdings and the pricing of unitized vehicles.

Information Technology

The Information Technology (IT) department is responsible for all systems and data used by asset managers. Data includes real-time data and news, supplied by such vendors as Bloomberg and Reuters, and historic data, for example, price and earnings histories for the universe in securities researched by the asset managers. Systems include back office investment accounting (which is the prime record for the asset manager's holdings), order management and dealing systems and fund analysis/ decision support systems.

External Service Providers

In addition to its own departments, asset managers are heavily reliant on the services of external companies. These include brokers, who provide security and market research as well as trade execution. Custodians are responsible for the management of the fund's physical assets (eg stock certificates, bank accounts etc) and are an important part of the overall service provided to clients. Performance measurers provide an 'independent' calculation of the fund's performance (although the underlying figures are generally provided by the asset management houses themselves, thus the performance figures cannot truly be independent).

CHAPTER 3

Implementing Modern Portfolio Theory

The entire fund management industry is based upon the precept that superior returns can be obtained by investing in a group of assets (ie a portfolio, or fund) rather than individual assets. By 'superior' it is held that a greater return can be obtained for an equivalent level of risk, or the same return can be gained for a lower risk. There are few who dispute this basic idea in theory, but the full practical implementation of Modern Portfolio Theory (MPT) is far from straightforward.

Having reviewed the theory, we will go on to look at the limitations imposed by the assumptions underlying these inter-related theories with a view to explaining the observed behaviour of asset managers.

Overview of Modern Portfolio Theory (MPT)

The following is a high level overview of MPT (Markowitz, 1952), the chief purpose of which is to establish the theory and assumptions surrounding it, in order that the difficulties of practical implementation are discussed within the framework of the theory. The reader is directed to the excellent book by Elton and Gruber[4] on this subject for a full description. This overview aims to illustrate the concepts behind the theory using numerical examples. A worthwhile exercise would be to replicate these examples using a spreadsheet in order to bring the theory to life. The areas of theory covered are Diversified Portfolios, the Capital Asset Pricing Model (CAPM) (Sharpe, 1964), the Arbitrage Pricing Theory (APT) (Ross, 1976) and the Efficient Markets Hypothesis.

---

[4] *Modern Portfolio Theory and Investment Analysis*, Elton and Gruber, Wiley 1995.

The Diversified Portfolio Concept

The basic idea behind MPT is that the set or 'universe' of securities representing the investment choice faced by an individual behave differently to each other. If, for example, the price of oil rises significantly then oil firms (for whom stocks will immediately be worth considerably more and whose margins may rise) will tend to offer better returns than firms for whom oil is a significant cost factor. When the price of oil falls, oil firms may well offer inferior returns when compared to others. The idea behind MPT is that, given the uncertainty surrounding factors such as the price of oil, one should spread one's capital across different investments in order that the portfolio is not completely exposed to an adverse piece of news affecting one security (or group of securities).

In the case of our oil firm, let's say that there are four possible scenarios in the next investment period, with each scenario having the same probability.

Oil Stock

Scenario	Effect on Stock Price
Oil Price Falls By 25%	−10.50%
Oil Price Falls By 10%	−0.67%
Oil Price Rises By 10%	5.67%
Oil Price Rises By 25%	13.50%
Expected Return	*2.00%*
Standard Deviation	*8.78%*

The expected return is simply the weighted average of the returns for each scenario (notice that +2.00% is not one of the possible outcomes). Since we do not, *a priori*, know what the outcome will be, the expected return is the best estimate that we can make of the return that we will receive from the oil stock. As you will have noticed, the actual returns, given that there are only these four scenarios, vary enormously (ranging from a negative return of 10.5% to a positive return of 13.5%). This variation is generally described as risk, the metric for which is nothing more complex than standard deviation. In this case the standard deviation is 8.78% (actually quite high given a mean of 2%!). It is this uncertainty that, according to MPT, we should avoid. Intuitively, any rational investor should minimize the risk of losing his hard earned capital, a 'given' being that he is taking a risk in the first place in order to benefit from an expected return.

We will now look at the returns expected from another firm, let's say a transport firm whose costs are very heavily influenced by the oil price.

Transport Stock

Scenario	Effect on Stock Price
Oil Price Falls By 25%	20.75%
Oil Price Falls By 10%	6.00%
Oil Price Rises By 10%	–3.50%
Oil Price Rises By 25%	–15.25%
Expected Return	*2.00%*
Standard Deviation	*13.18%*

Given that both have expected returns of 2.00% for the forthcoming period, at first glance we might be indifferent between the oil stock and the transport stock. If, however, we look at the riskiness (measured in terms of standard deviation) of the transport stock we can see that at 13.18% it is a lot higher than the oil stock. One of the precepts of MPT is that investors are risk averse, ie that they would prefer to have a lower risk of losing capital than a higher one (this is not unreasonable). Given this, the transport stock looks less attractive than the oil stock. Given the scenario painted, according to MPT our rational investor would choose the oil stock rather than the transport stock.

There is an alternative, however. By investing part of his funds in the oil stock and part in the transport stock the investor can achieve the following expected return profile.

Portfolio (60% Oil, 40% Transport)

Scenario	Effect on Stock Price
Oil Price Falls By 25%	2.00%
Oil Price Falls By 10%	2.00%
Oil Price Rises By 10%	2.00%
Oil Price Rises By 25%	2.00%
Expected Return	*2.00%*
Standard Deviation	*0.00%*

The startling aspect of this profile is that the expected 2% return is observed *whatever the economic scenario*, thereby giving a standard deviation, or risk figure, of 0%. Intuitively, this is correct: given that there are only four scenarios, and that we achieve 2% whatever happens, there is no risk associated with the 2% return. Of course, this situation is a little contrived, but empirically certain stocks are observed to react in the opposite way to others, thereby creating this type of opportunity. Graphically, the different investment options can be summarized as follows:

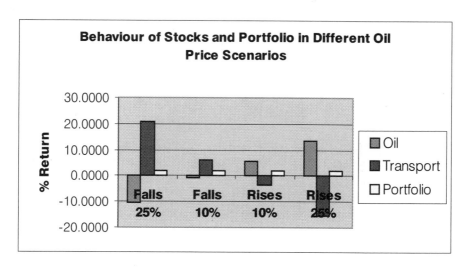

In a nutshell, this is the idea behind MPT; that by combining securities in a portfolio, one can drastically reduce the overall risk of investing in assets.

These assets may have very high variance individually, but because they behave differently to each other they can be combined to produce a portfolio offering, in MPT terms, superior expected returns.

Covariance Analysis

One way of explaining this 'superior' portfolio expected return is in terms of the covariance of returns between the oil stock and the transport stock. This covariance is calculated using the standard formula:

$$\sigma_{oil,\,transport} = (E(r_{oil}) - E(\overline{r})) \times (E(r_{transport}) - E(\overline{r}))$$

and in this case is −115.9, a high negative figure[5]. By converting it to a correlation coefficient (which does not change this metric's properties, but simply makes the figure more useful for comparative purposes by scaling it in the range −1 (perfect negative correlation) to +1 (perfect positive correlation)) using the following standard formula:

$$\rho_{oil,\,transport} = \frac{\sigma_{oil,\,transport}}{\sigma_{oil}\,\sigma_{transport}}$$

here giving a correlation coefficient of −1, ie a perfect negative correlation.

The pragmatic use of this covariance measure is, potentially, as a key input when fund managers are considering whether or not to buy stocks not currently held in their portfolio. The fund manager, following the MPT argument, would assess whether the security would reduce the overall risk of the portfolio (while keeping the return the same or increasing it). An initial guide would be to calculate the covariance between the stock under consideration and the portfolio held.

To illustrate this point, let's consider a new portfolio with the profile specified below and consider whether or not to include an additional stock in this portfolio.

---

[5] Incidentally, the portfolio standard deviation can also be derived using the formula:
$$\sigma^2 = A^2\sigma^2_{oil} + B^2\sigma^2_{transport} + 2A.B\sigma_{oil,\,transport}$$
which here is
$$\sigma^2 = 0.36(77.3) + 0.16(173.8) + 2(0.6\text{x}0.4) \times - 115.9$$
$$= 27.83 + 27.81 - 55.64 = 0.$$

Existing Portfolio

Scenario	Effect on Portfolio Value
Oil Price Falls By 25%	2.50%
Oil Price Falls By 10%	3.00%
Oil Price Rises By 10%	3.00%
Oil Price Rises By 25%	3.50%
Expected Return	3.00%
Standard Deviation	0.125%

We'll consider two stocks, firstly a retailer having to pay higher transport costs in the event of a rise, but not benefiting from an oil price fall, and secondly a bank, which is very insensitive to changes in the price of oil.

Retail Stock

Scenario	Effect on Stock Price
Oil Price Falls By 25%	4.00%
Oil Price Falls By 10%	3.50%
Oil Price Rises By 10%	2.50%
Oil Price Rises By 25%	2.00%
Expected Return	3.00%
Standard Deviation	0.79%
Covariance with Existing Portfolio	−0.25
Correlation Coefficient	−0.89

Bank

Scenario	Effect on Stock Price
Oil Price Falls By 25%	2.965%
Oil Price Falls By 10%	3.000%
Oil Price Rises By 10%	3.015%
Oil Price Rises By 25%	3.020%
Expected Return	3.000%
Standard Deviation	0.0004%
Covariance with Existing Portfolio	0.0069
Correlation Coefficient	0.9042

On the basis of the Bank stock offering the same return for a lower risk, one might be tempted to include this stock rather than the Retailer. Additionally, the Retailer has a higher risk than either the portfolio or the Bank stock. However, MPT would suggest that, by looking at the covariance between each proposed stock and the existing portfolio, that the Retailer would be preferable. This is because it behaves differently in each scenario to the portfolio, ie it has a negative covariance (and correlation coefficient) with it.

By incorporating the Retailer into the portfolio we can achieve the following.

Existing Portfolio (60%) + Retailer (40%)

Scenario	*Effect on Portfolio Value*
Oil Price Falls By 25%	3.10%
Oil Price Falls By 10%	3.20%
Oil Price Rises By 10%	2.80%
Oil Price Rises By 25%	2.90%
Expected Return	*3.00%*
Standard Deviation	*0.16%*

This significantly reduced portfolio risk associated with the same return is despite the fact that the Retailer had, in itself, a higher risk than the portfolio.

If we included the Bank stock instead, then the following would have been observed.

Existing Portfolio (60%) + Bank (40%)

Scenario	*Effect on Portfolio Value*
Oil Price Falls By 25%	2.686%
Oil Price Falls By 10%	3.000%
Oil Price Rises By 10%	3.006%
Oil Price Rises By 25%	3.308%
Expected Return	*3.00%*
Standard Deviation	*0.22%*

Thus a smaller, but still very significant, reduction in risk is achieved through the inclusion of the Bank rather than the Retailer. If the fund manager were forced to choose, according to MPT he would include the Retailer, rather than the bank stock. In practice, a bank stock would almost certainly be included in a portfolio of equities as well, particularly if it offered the fund manager a risk reducing opportunity. Here, the inclusion of the bank stock in the new portfolio (ie including the Retailer) would result in the following set of expected returns.

New Portfolio (60%) + Bank (40%)

Scenario	Effect on Portfolio Value
Oil Price Falls By 25%	3.046%
Oil Price Falls By 10%	3.120%
Oil Price Rises By 10%	2.886%
Oil Price Rises By 25%	2.948%
Expected Return	*3.000%*
Standard Deviation	*0.090%*

Thus the overall risk of the portfolio has been reduced once more, while maintaining the expected return of 3%. In fact this process of portfolio risk reduction will tend to continue as stocks are added. At its limit (ie with an infinite number of stocks – or the entire market), all that will remain will be the overall market risk (as represented by, for example, the FTSE 100, S&P 500 index etc). This market risk cannot be diversified away. This should be intuitive – by investing in the market one is taking on both the potential upside gain in terms of expected returns as well as the downside risk, ie the risk of capital loss.

The focus in the above analysis has been on optimizing the portfolio by attempting to reduce the level of risk for the same level of return. MPT states that the portfolio that we ended up with is 'superior' to any of the other combinations that we looked at. Of course, there will be combinations of securities that have a higher or lower expected return, with higher or lower associated risks. Where there is a higher return with a higher risk, we cannot say whether this is better or worse than a portfolio with a lower return with a lower associated level of risk. This is since this judgment is a subjective one on behalf of each investor, known as his risk preference. The set of choices available to an investor can be plotted as follows, with the expected return on the Y axis and the risk (standard deviation) on the X axis.

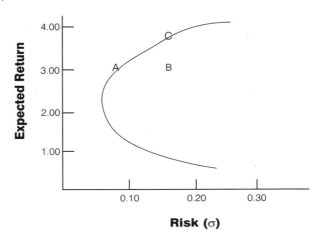

Risk (σ)

Efficient Frontier Analysis

The series of values on the curved line is known as the 'efficient frontier', the idea being that there is neither a higher return available for a given level of risk, nor a lower risk for the same return. Point A plots the risk against return for the final portfolio that we ended up with, having added both the Retailer and the Bank. Point B is the portfolio before the addition of the banking stock. In MPT terms this is not an efficient portfolio since the same return is available for a lower risk (eg at point A). At point C we have a different situation; here the expected return is higher, but at a higher risk. In this type of scenario it is left to the investor to decide whether the additional return is warranted by the additional risk of loss of capital.

Given a very large number of potential investments, how many stocks should a fund manager hold in his portfolio? Elton and Gruber analysed the average portfolio variance for portfolios consisting of different numbers of stocks listed on the New York Stock Exchange.

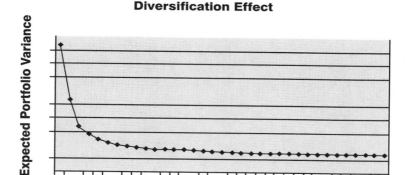

This shows a diminishing marginal diversification effect through the addition of new securities to the portfolio. Fund managers tend to have a minimum of 15 stocks in their portfolio, but will hold more securities if the overall value of the fund is higher. Certainly by the time 15 stocks have been included, a very great proportion of *specific* risk (ie risk associated with the holding of individual securities) has been diversified away as a result of the differing behaviour of securities given different market conditions.

MPT makes the fairly strong assertion that there is never any mileage in holding individual securities, since these holdings are 'inferior' on a risk/return ratio basis to combinations of groups of assets. In MPT terms there is no reward for holding diversifiable risk, since the rational investor would take the opportunity to diversify any specific risk away. The result of this is that the fund manager is left with only the market risk (and of course its associated level of return).

CAPM and the Market Price of Risk

The theory that investors are not rewarded (ie there is no additional expected return available) for holding any diversifiable risk, is taken to its logical limit in the Capital Asset Pricing Model (CAPM). This model is based on the premise that all investors will hold portfolios which are invested in every single asset in existence. The rationale behind this is that, if an investible asset is not included, then an opportunity for diversification, and therefore risk reduction, has been missed. This theoretical 'market portfolio' is weighted according to the relative overall market values (for example the market capitalization of equities or prior charge capital for bonds) of each asset. Thus if the investible universe consisted of only the following five assets (rather than the actual virtually infinite number), with the following market values, then the theory suggests that all investors' portfolios will have the following weightings.

Asset	Total Market Value (£ '000,000s)	Market Portfolio Weight
Vodafone	62,000	27.6
Nintendo	55,000	24.4
BSkyB 8% 2041	45,000	20.0
Manhattan Real Estate	38,000	16.9
Global Repurchase Agreement 4%	25,000	11.1
Total	225,000	100.0

This theory has interesting implications, one of which is that holders of any portfolio with a different construction to the market portfolio will hold a sub-optimal combination (ie there will be a portfolio available offering a lower risk for the same expected return, or a higher expected return for the same risk). This would result in consistent underperformance, when compared to the market portfolio, in the long run. Another is that assets are correctly valued (otherwise holders of this portfolio would find themselves holding the wrong proportions of assets when the price returned to its correct level).

Deriving the CAPM

The final building block of CAPM is to introduce the concept of investor risk preference. According to the theory, investors will combine the market portfolio outlined above with a risk-free asset (eg a short term government debt instrument[6]). The proportion of the risk-free asset held will increase the greater the investor's risk aversion (if he is totally risk averse, by definition he will hold 100% of his capital in the risk-free asset). We can layer these combinations on top of the efficient frontier diagram that we saw earlier.

[6]   Short term to eliminate inflation risk, government to eliminate default risk.

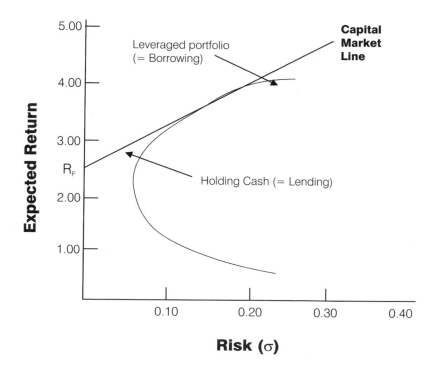

Risk (σ)

Thus by introducing the concept of a risk-free asset, new 'superior' portfolios[7] are introduced into the equation. At the tangent of the straight line (capital market line) and the curved efficient frontier without lending and borrowing, is the optimal market portfolio. This combination of assets will obviously change if the risk-free rate changes (since the straight line will touch the curve at a different point).

This takes us closer to understanding the CAPM, which is concerned with pricing market risk, ie determining what additional expected return is required for additional market risk. Since, in this model, the only risk considered by a rational investor is market risk (ie the risk of the overall market portfolio), we need to measure each security's risk in these terms. This measure is generally referred to as the Beta (β) of each security, measuring the degree to which securities move in line with the market. In our much simplified investible universe, the betas of each security might be as follows.

[7] 'Superior' because all combinations lie to the left of the efficient frontier, ie they offer a higher return for a given level of risk (except at the tangential point where they are equal).

Asset	Total Market Value (£ '000,000's)	Market Portfolio Weight	Beta
Vodafone	62,000	27.6	1.12
Nintendo	55,000	24.4	1.24
BSkyB 8% 2041	45,000	20.0	0.91
Manhattan Real Estate	38,000	16.9	0.61
Global Repurchase Agreement 4%	25,000	11.1	0.93
Total	225,000	100.0	1.00

This profile might be expected, equities having a higher market risk, and property having the least sensitivity to overall market movements (since rents etc tend to be fixed for relatively long periods and property prices tend to be fairly stable over time). The CAPM states that those securities with a higher beta should offer a higher expected return since they have a higher level of market risk. This concept can be demonstrated using our small example.

Assuming that investors are only rewarded (in terms of expected return) for assuming market risk, we can analyse each security as follows.

If the market return in our universe specified above is 3.5% and the risk free rate is 2.5%, this would imply that each of our five securities would offer the following expected returns E(R).

Asset	Total Market Value (£ '000,000's)	Market Portfolio Weight	Beta	E(R)
Vodafone	62,000	27.6	1.12	3.62
Nintendo	55,000	24.4	1.24	3.74
BSkyB 8% 2041	45,000	20.0	0.91	3.41
Manhattan Real Estate	38,000	16.9	0.61	3.11
Global Repurchase Agreement 4%	25,000	11.1	0.93	3.43
Total	225,000	100.0	1.00	3.50

This example hopefully brings out the close relationship between the security's beta, the expected return of the market and the weight that each security represents in the market portfolio. The key elements here are as follows:

▶ The higher the weighting a security has, the greater will be its influence on the market return

▶ The higher its beta, or risk measured in terms of market risk, the greater must be the compensating expected return

▶ The higher the risk free rate, the higher will be the required expected return

This relationship is summarized graphically in the security market line, as follows.

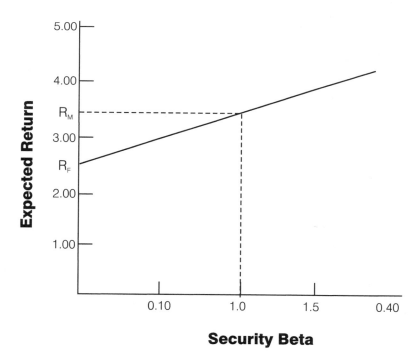

Security Beta

Security Market Line

Simple as it looks, this security market line describes the expected return for *all* assets and combinations of assets in portfolios according to CAPM. Thus we simply need to calculate the beta of the asset or portfolio, and we can derive the expected return from the security market line.

APT: An Alternative Pricing Theorem

Introduction

At its simplest level the Arbitrage Pricing Theorem (APT) is based on the premise that two items with equivalent characteristics cannot simultaneously be priced differently (otherwise arbitrageurs would step in and simultaneously sell at the high price and buy at the low price making a risk-free profit).

Similarly to the CAPM, the APT is concerned with the pricing of risks pertaining to securities. Unlike the CAPM it suggests that there is more than one factor (ie market returns in the CAPM) affecting security returns. The APT is implemented by identifying factors affecting stock returns (such as inflation, interest rates etc) and calculating the sensitivity of individual securities to each factor. This sensitivity is analogous to the Beta in the CAPM and is used by the APT to calculate an expected return compensating investors for their risky exposure to these factors in combination. By setting all but one of the sensitivities to zero, the model can be used to calculate the return required for taking on the risk of each factor.

APT Structure

APT proposes that security returns are driven by a linear relationship to a series of indices (ie a multi-index model), rather than the mean variance framework of the CAPM. If we assume (and this is a strong assumption) that we can source indices that will accurately reflect the factors influencing the returns on securities, then we can set up a model for the return of each security in the following form:

$$R_{SECURITY} = \alpha_{SECURITY} + \beta_{Index1}(index1) + \beta_{Index2}(index2) + ... \beta_{IndexN}(IndexN) + e_{SECURITY}$$

where: $\alpha_{SECURITY}$ is the return due to stock specific factors

β_{Index} is the sensitivity of a each particular security to an index

IndexN is the element of return attributable to a particular factor (as represented by an index)

e_{SECURITY} is a Gaussian white noise error process with mean zero

APT proposes that this model be applied to all securities in order to calculate their expected returns. All of the indices are the same for each security: it is the security's sensitivity to changes in the index which is unique to each security. Two examples of APT models are as follows.

NYSE Stock Returns 1931-79: Sharpe (1982)

Factor	Element of Overall Return Attributable to Factor
Stock Attributes (α type factors)	
Security Beta (with respect to S&P 500 Index)	5.36
Dividend Yield	0.24
Company Size (in Market Value terms)	−5.56
Security Bond Beta (to long Government Bond)	−0.12
Residual Alpha (all other stock specific factors)	−2.00

Factor	Element of Overall Return Attributable to Factor
Sector Membership (β type factors)	
Basic Industries	1.65
Capital Goods	0.16
Construction	−1.59
Consumer Goods	−0.18
Energy	6.28
Finance	−1.48
Transport	−0.57
Utilities	−2.62

Factor Sensitivities for APT: Burmeister and McElroy (1988)

Factor	Element of Overall Return Attributable to Factor
Average Return Due to Stock Specific Factors (α)	0.00224
Default Risk (= Government – Corporate Bond Returns)	–1.330
Time Premium (for Lending Longer)	0.558
Deflation	2.286
Change in Expected Sales	0.935

Concept

Similarly to CAPM, APT assumes that investors will hold well diversified portfolios. The implication of this is that the residual, or stock specific, risk will tend to zero, leaving simply the sensitivity weighted economic factors specified in the multi-index model used. Let us simplify the global securities market into three investible categories, and consider three well diversified portfolios invested in these categories with the following sensitivities to two factors, interest rate changes and industrial productivity changes.

Portfolio/Category	$E(R)$	$\beta_{INTEREST\ RATES}$	$\beta_{PRODUCTIVITY}$
UK Equities	12	0.8	1.2
Overseas Equities	16	1.6	1.8
Bonds	10	1.2	0.6

APT theory states that all portfolios must be a function of this model, otherwise an arbitrage opportunity would exist. To illustrate this, let us consider a global 'fund of funds' portfolio invested in equal proportions in each portfolio/category specified above.

Portfolio/Category	Weight	E(R)	$\beta_{INTEREST\ RATES}$	$\beta_{PRODUCTIVITY}$
UK Equities	33.33%	12	0.8	1.2
Overseas Equities	33.33%	16	1.6	1.8
Bonds	33.33%	10	1.2	0.6
Overall Fund of Funds	100.00%	12.67	1.2	1.2

APT argues that if another portfolio existed with, for the sake of example, the following profile.

Fund of Funds II	100.00%	14.33	1.2	1.2

then a risk-free profit would be available to arbitrageurs, who could fund the purchase of units of the higher yielding Fund of Funds II by selling units of our original Fund of Funds short. In this case they would earn a risk-free 1.67% expected return. According to APT, this arbitrage will continue until Fund of Funds II was offering the same expected return of 12.67%.

Thus APT is really making the same fundamental statement as CAPM theory, that there is an equilibrium level of security prices dictated by the level of risk associated with each security. The chief difference between the two is that CAPM pricing is based on the security's co-movement with the overall market, whereas APT pricing is based on each security's sensitivity to changes in an unspecified series of factors influencing the market. The specification of factors in APT is left to individual market analysts.

The Efficient Markets Hypothesis (EMH)

The Efficient Markets Hypothesis (EMH) essentially states that all securities' market prices fairly reflect their value to investors. The implications of this mainly surround the availability and analysis of available information pertaining to the future values of securities. Fama (1970) distinguishes three forms of the EMH, as follows.

Weak Form	All data regarding the security's behaviour contained in historical prices is reflected in the current security price
Semi-Strong Form	Where all publicly available information is reflected in the security price

Strong Form	Where all information, whether publicly available or not, is included in the security price (even insider dealers would not be able to make a profit if this version held)

Empirical studies have lent support to the semi-strong form of the EMH. Another implication of the EMH is that, independent of which form of it is believed in, all market players (brokers, analysts, fund managers, private investors) interpret the available information in the same way. Additionally, it is also implicit that all market players receive this information at the same time.

Empirical Departures from Modern Portfolio Theory

Some of the assumptions underlying MPT and associated theorems such as CAPM, APT and EMH are somewhat removed from the real world of investment. The following table gives a fairly comprehensive list of these assumptions, the real-life situation and the impact that this has on the practical implementation of the theory.

General

Assumption	Real Life Situation	Impact
Accurate and consistent pricing of assets through time	Distortion and artificial protection of markets through government intervention and anti-competitive collusion	Inaccurate allocations of capital through weightings being calculated from inflated prices for some asset classes (eg third world debt having an unaccounted for international agency bail-out option instead of default)

CAPM

Real Life Situation	Assumption	Impact
No transaction costs	Existence of transaction costs	More costly to move in and out of security positions

CAPM *(cont.)*

Assumption	*Real Life Situation*	*Impact*
Infinite divisibility of securities	Securities not infinitely divisible (eg Equity Board Lot Sizes)	Difficult to establish portfolios containing large numbers of holdings unless funds very large in size (in which case other difficulties ensue)
Can define all future possible 'states of the world'	Difficult to define a comprehensive set of all possible outcomes[8]	Makes it difficult to apply CAPM to the real world
Can use expected returns for each 'state of the world'	Expected returns generally based on historic data, rather than forward looking forecasting techniques. Data may well not exist historically for each scenario.	Previous data not really comprehensive enough, in terms of possible scenarios to be used in practice
Can assign a probability to each possible outcome	No real scientific way of calculating these probabilities	Investment directors could not be entirely confident of strategy models based on 'guesstimates'
Can define investor risk preference	Difficult to quantify in practice	Cannot specify precise mix of market portfolio and risk free assets for each investor

---

[8] Even if there were only six different factors which influence asset prices, and each of these only had four possible outcomes, the number of different combinations, each of which would need to have a probability assigned to it, would be $4 \times 6! = 2,880$.

CAPM *(cont.)*

Assumption	Real Life Situation	Impact
All investors have same requirements	Different investors have different growth, income and tax requirements	Same portfolio mix of assets will not meet requirements of all investors
All assets available for investment	Limited liquidity in many assets (eg bonds bought and held, private companies and private property)	Reduces diversification opportunity upon which CAPM is based

EMH

Assumption	Real Life Situation	Impact
'Public' information available to all market players at the same time (semi-strong version of EMH)	Larger investment houses will receive, and be able to assimilate, data faster than smaller scale players	Larger houses have an information advantage

APT

Assumption	Real Life Situation	Impact
Funds can be sold short	May not be possible, since would necessitate the borrowing of units of funds to deliver when selling short	Arbitrageurs less able to correct mis-pricing of funds

APT *(cont.)*

Assumption	*Real Life Situation*	*Impact*
Indices available which accurately reflect all factors which might affect security returns	Indices may not be available, or may not closely enough track the factor included in the model (eg inflationary expectations)	Undermines the power of any APT model

In addition to these fairly understandable departures from MPT, there is an additional observed tendency for fund managers to favour their own, 'home' markets (eg UK fund managers investing disproportionately in the UK equity market). This has been termed the 'home bias' puzzle, and can be clearly illustrated by the following chart showing the difference between the mean distribution of actual pension fund investment in equities (the 'WM Mean Distribution of Assets') and a market capitalization weighted distribution (the 'MSCI Index')[9].

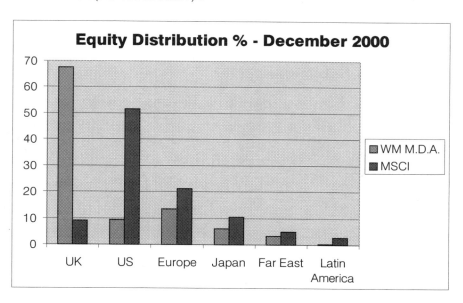

[9] Benchmarks and indices are covered in detail in the next chapter.

41

This dramatic departure from the principles of MPT – that all investors should invest in equal proportions of the same market (ie market capitalization weighted) portfolio – has been the subject of considerable research. An overview of this research is provided in Appendix V.

Which Elements of Modern Portfolio Theory are Actually Used In Practice?

Having ripped these well-established theories to shreds, it is important to emphasize that despite their many simplifying assumptions, MPT still justifiably provides the cornerstones of portfolio management. In particular, the adoption of the principle of portfolio diversification has (generally) enabled fund managers to offer investors returns that are consistently higher than the 'risk-free' rate (a good proxy for this being three month LIBOR[10]). With regard to CAPM, it does appear that the number of different security holdings tends to increase as the fund size increases, ie fund managers are diversifying as far as they possibly can. This supports the assertion that CAPM could be viewed as being implemented as far as possible given real life constraints. This observed behaviour is presumably due to obstacles such as minimum transaction costs (which would prohibit certain sizes of holdings) and granularity of asset holdings being removed as the smallest holdings increase in size. Ross's (1976) Arbitrage Price Theory (APT) introduced the concept of weighted factor models determining asset prices. This concept provides one of the bases for modern econometric modelling.

As we will see when reviewing the techniques employed in portfolio management, there are strong roots in these theories. The difficulty in forecasting future events has never been harder than in the modern world; as a minimum MPT enables fund managers to exercise a degree of control over the risks involved.

---

[10] London Inter-Bank Offered Rate, generally viewed as a benchmark for interest rate levels generally.

CHAPTER 4

Benchmarks and Indices

Introduction

In most industries companies utilize comparative measures in order to assess the amount of risk that they are taking and how well they are performing.

Performance is generally thought of in terms of monetary amounts made or lost (ie profits and losses). Risk is generally thought of in terms of the risk of losing money; this being a composite function of the amount of money at risk and the probability of losing this monetary amount. These monetary amounts can also be expressed in terms of returns, by dividing the amounts made by the amount of capital used to generate these amounts and are generally referred to as Return on Capital Employed (ROCE). These returns can be used to compare returns available from different projects that the firm might undertake. Further analysis may be carried out to assess the likelihood of achieving these returns with a view to selecting the project with the best chance of generating the highest return. The ROCE figures might also be used to compare the performance of companies within a particular industry by comparing the ROCE for a company with a benchmark ROCE, perhaps calculated as the average ROCE for that industry. It might also be used to compare alternative investments such as an interest rate available from bank deposits. Depending upon the purpose of the analysis, potential investors may use the ROCE comparison to choose between companies within a particular sector or to decide between investing in equities or leaving their money on deposit.

Within the fund management industry investors similarly need information in order to assess the performance and risk of a fund. Fund managers themselves also need to know what their returns are, compared to alternatives, in order to get feedback on the success or otherwise of their investment strategies.

Benchmarks, and their constituent indices, play a pivotal role in this analysis. In fact one could argue that funds exist only in terms of their relativity to their benchmark. The performance of the fund is assessed by comparing the return of the fund against the return of an appropriate benchmark. The result of this analysis is termed the *relative performance* of the fund and is the main measure used to assess the skill of a fund manager. This relative performance is very important since it expresses how well the fund manager has done *given that* capital has been allocated to his fund. Thus if an investor has purchased units in a UK equity fund, and UK equities fall over a given period of observation, he may chide himself for having invested in UK equities (ie having made an asset allocation decision to invest in UK equities) but will also want to know how well the fund manager has done relative to his peers (ie other UK equity funds in which the investor could have placed his capital).

By way of example, let us say that UK equity returns, as measured by an appropriate index such as the FT-A All Share Index, have fallen by 10% in a year, while UK interest rates (as measured by using an interest-rate index such as 12 month LIBOR) are 4.5 % per annum. Finally a particular fund manager's portfolio of UK equities has fallen by 5%. Armed with this information we can answer some questions regarding the fund's performance but it is key that we are clear about what question it is we are asking.

Thus, the question: 'How well did I do by selecting UK equities as an investment type?' could be answered by comparing the performance of UK equities to an alternative such as 'Cash' where we earn interest on cash at the going rate. The question could be answered as follows: 'You did badly; you chose an investment that lost 10% of your capital over the year when you could have earned 4.5%'. Slightly more formally, the answer could be expressed as 'Your relative return was -14.5%'. This is a very different question to that of 'How well did the fund manager do?' where we could answer: 'He did well. He only lost 5% of the fund's value when the market in general fell by 10%', or 'His relative return was +5%'. The manager outperformed because his mandate was to invest in UK equities, ie he did not have an opportunity to invest in any other market.

The risk of a fund is also measured by comparing it to its benchmark. This can be carried out in two main ways, by comparing the historic returns of the fund and its benchmark and by comparing the composition of the fund with that of its benchmark. By comparing the composition of the fund with its benchmark, questions such as 'Relative to the benchmark, how high is our exposure to telecommunication/Argentinian/Yen denominated securities?'. This type of analysis gives an idea of the specific factor risks that the fund is exposed to. An overall measure can be provided by calculating the standard deviation of the fund's performance relative to the benchmark, this being termed 'tracking error'. A high tracking error implies a relatively high probability of the overall fund return being significantly lower than that of its benchmark (as well as a good chance that the fund could significantly outperform). The fund might therefore really only be of interest to investors with a relatively high risk appetite.

Benchmarks

The concept of benchmarking funds is one of the most fundamental in the fund management industry. It also seems generally to be rather misunderstood, hence the laboured explanation here.

A fund's benchmark is set by the trustees with the intention of using it to monitor the level of risk taken by the fund manager, this being measured by his deviation from benchmark weights. The weights used represent market exposure ie what proportion of the fund is exposed to the risks and returns of each market. It is this exposure that the fund manager is most interested in, whether sourced from underlying assets such as equities or bonds or derivatives. The benchmark also enables the trustee to assess the fund manager's performance through the calculation of a relative return figure.

Following on from the previous chapter, in CAPM terms the benchmark could be viewed as the consensus view of what constitutes the realistic investible universe for the fund. According to the CAPM theory, therefore, the fund manager should invest funds proportionately according to the relative market values of all of the assets implicitly specified by the benchmark. He would also adjust the fund's holdings for the client's 'risk appetite' by investing a proportion of the fund in a 'risk-free' asset such as a US Government Treasury Bill.

This, however, implies that the world's wealth is currently distributed efficiently (ie that in general investors are allocating their capital to those companies issuing equity and debt offering the best risk adjusted returns). Nearly all fund managers would not invest in the entire asset universe in this way. They would not subscribe to the theory that capital is efficiently allocated and would, therefore, take 'bets' against the benchmark where they felt that allocation was inefficient (ie securities are mispriced in the light of available information and analysis). From a 'risk appetite' perspective, in practice the Trustees (acting on behalf of the beneficiaries of the fund) would set a series of constraints on the fund to keep allocation of funds within a given range. The higher the clients' 'risk appetite', the greater the permitted deviation from the fund's benchmark.

An example of a real-life pension fund benchmark, as published by specialist companies such as World Markets (WM) or Combined Actuarial Portfolio Service (CAPS), is provided below.

WM Mean Distribution of Assets (December 2000)

▨ UK Equities	▨ US Equities
☐ Japan Equities	☐ Europe ex-UK Equities
■ Far East ex-Japan Equities	▨ Property
▨ UK Bonds	▨ Overseas Bonds
■ Cash	

These benchmark weights are calculated through surveying as many similar funds as possible to give an average weight for all funds in a particular category. Thus a mean distribution of assets will be calculated for all funds in the same 'peer group' (eg life, pension or unit trust funds).

Indices

Indices can be viewed as proxies for particular markets, for example, the FT All Share index being used as a proxy for the UK Equity Market. They are used for two main purposes, one being to provide a guide to how the market for which it is a proxy is performing. Thus, if the FT All Share starts the month on 3,000 and ends on 3,300, it could be said that the UK market has gone up by 10%. However, it is important to choose the most appropriate index. If, for example, the fund was investing in larger capitalization stocks, it would be more relevant to use the FTSE 100 index of the largest 100 UK stocks by company size.

The other use of indices is to facilitate a lower level of analysis by providing fund managers with the constituents of the indices (and, therefore, by implication the security level benchmark).

Roles of the Benchmark

A fund's benchmark fulfils several functions, detailed below.

Fund Structure Guideline

The benchmark, with its associated constraints, gives the fund manager his guidelines for managing the fund. It could be viewed as the fund manager's 'neutral' position, ie if he felt that an asset category was correctly priced with normal growth prospects. The fund manager will base his investment decisions on this structure, overweighting asset categories with good growth potential, and underweighting categories that he feels are overpriced. Given that the benchmark data is publicly available, it is this over- or underweighting that provides the source of the fund manager's 'added value'.

Benchmarks are generally specified by the Trustees at a fairly general level, giving the fund manager a guideline with regard to the top level allocation (eg equity, bond and cash split), and usually an allocation to global equity regions (UK, US, Europe ex-UK etc). This could be referred to as an *explicit benchmark*. However, the fund manager needs a further breakdown to enable him to monitor his risk (ie over- or underweightedness against the benchmark) at a lower level than that provided (eg individual countries within the Europe ex-UK region). In order to do this, the fund manager might agree a set of indices with the Trustees that accurately represent the benchmarks at a lower level. Thus he could agree the following indices.

Region	Representative Index
UK	FT All Share
US	S&P 500
Europe ex-UK	MSCI Europe ex-UK
Japan	Nikkei 225
Asia Pacific ex-Japan	MSCI Asia Pacific ex-Japan
Latin America	IFC Latin American Index

This enables the fund manager to infer his neutral position weights at a more detailed level (ie his *implied benchmark*). Thus if the overall benchmark allocation to Europe ex-UK was 16% and the weight of France within the MSCI Europe ex-UK index was 40%, the weight of France in the overall benchmark can be calculated as 6.4%. If the weights of the constituent indices are provided at stock level, then the fund manager can calculate the weight of his implicit benchmark down to individual security level.

For fixed interest funds (or parts or 'segments' of funds), similar data is available, the only real differences being the different asset classes used to break the fund down (eg currency of issue and 'maturity bucket') and market exposure being presented in weighted duration terms. These concepts are explained in detail in the Fixed Interest Management chapter.

Performance Comparison

Performance analysis is very important in the asset management industry. It provides a feedback mechanism for the fund manager, telling him how he is doing, and why (indeed a fund manger's remuneration often heavily relies on his fund's performance). Performance analysis also gives the Trustees (acting on behalf of the client) an idea of how his investment is doing compared to alternative investment opportunities (especially other fund managers). If the fund's performance consistently underperforms alternatives, Trustees may move the funds elsewhere. The performance of the benchmark is carried out by calculating the weighted[11] performance of the agreed series of indices, thereby giving the performance of the benchmark. The fund manager can then compare the overall performance of his fund with the benchmark's performance (which would be the same as the fund manager's performance if he remained neutral in all markets), giving him his *relative return*. This important measure essentially shows how much value the fund manager has added through taking bets against the benchmark.

Examples of Fund vs Benchmark Analysis

The fund versus benchmark analysis is the main type of analysis used by fund managers on a day to day basis. Ideally he would like to see his fund broken down in a number of ways, but in practice it may be difficult to source all of the data required. In particular, it is not always possible to get hold of index constituent data at stock level, making the levels of analysis possible entirely dependent upon the level of granularity at which the data is available.

Equities

For equity fund managers, a geographical analysis has been a traditional way of breaking a portfolio down. A typical analysis might be as follows.

Fund:	Global Growth	Current Value:		£260,450,596	
	Current Fund Weight	Benchmark Weight	'Bet' Position	Model Rebalancing	Action
UK	54.6	54.8	-2.0	52.8	−1.8
US	18.3	17.5	+1.5	19.0	+0.7
Japan	8.2	9.1	−1.0	8.1	−0.1
Europe ex-UK	12.2	14.1	−1.5	12.6	+0.4
Far East ex-Japan	6.1	4.0	+3.0	7.0	+0.9
Latin America	0.6	0.5	+0.0	0.5	−0.1
Total	100.0	100.0	0.0	100.0	0.0

---

[11] Weighted using the percentages allocated on average by the fund manager's rival managers.

Thus the model position is created by taking bets around the fund's benchmark, showing the fund manager's desired position in percentage exposure terms. This is then compared to the current weight in the fund to give the 'rebalancing action' percentage to buy and sell. By using the fund's overall value, the fund manager can then calculate the amounts that need to be invested or disinvested from each market (eg by buying or selling OEICs) to achieve his required position. An obvious, but important, note is that this is a zero sum game, ie investment in one area needs to be funded by disinvestment from another. An example of a full rebalancing system is given in the Systems and Data Environment chapter.

Bonds

Fixed interest managers' exposures are very similar, in that the fund's exposure to each market is compared to the exposure of the benchmark. The main difference is that bond fund managers look at a weighted duration figure, which combines the percentage exposure to each market with the sensitivity of bonds to changes in interest rates, which is the main factor influencing bond prices. This is covered in detail in the Fixed Interest Management chapter, but the following example gives an idea of the type of analysis used.

Fund:	*Global Bond*	*Current Value:*		£5,370,263,610	
	Current Fund Weighted Duration	*Benchmark Weighted Duration*	*'Bet'*	*Model Position*	*Rebalancing Action*
US Dollar	2.3	2.0	+0.2	2.2	–0.1
Euro	1.7	1.5	+0.2	1.7	0.0
Japanese Yen	1.2	1.3	–0.1	1.2	0.0
Sterling	1.4	1.2	+0.1	1.3	–0.1
Total	6.6	6.0	+0.4	6.4	–0.2

It is interesting to note that fixed interest rebalancing is not a zero sum game. The model fund ends up 0.4 years longer than the benchmark. This is perfectly normal and simply means that the fund manager is more bullish than his peers eg he expects interest rates to generally fall and/or demand for bonds to generally increase. Similarly to equities, the fund manager can calculate the amount of a particular bond to buy or sell to rebalance his portfolio using the following formula:

$$No\ min\ al = \frac{Weighted\_Duration\_Required}{Bond\_Duration\_x\_Dirty\_Price} \text{ x Fund Value}$$

eg a £15,000,000 fund manager has identified an attractive bond in which he wants to have an exposure of 0.2 years weighted duration. The bond's dirty price (ie including accrued interest) is 105.62 and its modified duration is 4.2 years. The nominal he needs to buy to achieve the 0.2 years weighted duration can be calculated as follows:

$$\frac{0.2}{4.2 \times (105.62/100)} \times 15,000,000 = 984,060$$

Currency

Currency management is carried out on an overlay basis ie currency exposure/risk is calculated from the underlying securities in the fund (eg sterling exposure is the sum of percentage exposures to UK equities, UK bonds and UK property holdings) and managed separately.

Underlying Asset Class	Asset Weight	Currency Weight	Currency
UK Equities	55.3	75.0	Sterling
Property	1.7		
UK Bonds	11.5		
Cash Sterling	6.5		
US Equities	5.7	8.0	US Dollar
US Bonds	2.3		
Japan Equities	6.4	6.4	Yen
Europe ex-UK Equities	10.6	10.6	Euro
Total	100.0	100.0	Total

Calculations

Much time and effort is spent in fund management houses in calculating benchmark and index positions for their funds. This is because the published data is generally not quite in the format that the fund manager needs it. Two main types of adjustments are described below.

Calculation of implicit, lower level benchmark from indices

This is a fairly simple exercise, but an important one since it allows the fund manager to look at his relative position against the benchmark at a much lower level than would otherwise be possible. In a very simplified example, let us say that the fund manager has a mandate to manage a fund investing in UK and US equities. The fund's benchmark is in proportions of 60% in the UK and 40% in the US, these percentages being set by the Trustee. Let us also say that the indices used to proxy the UK and US market are the fictitious 'FTSE 3' and 'S&P 4' indices, with three and four holdings respectively.

	'FTSE 3'			'S&P 4'	
	Market Cap (£'000,000s)	*Index Weight*		*Market Cap*	*Index Weight*
BT	37,365	12.5	Ford	28,868	7.7
Glaxo	119,385	39.8	Microsoft	166,199	44.3
Vodafone	143,175	47.7	Texaco	22,543	6.0
			Wal-Mart	157,569	42.0
Total	*299,925*	*100.0*	*Total*	*375,179*	*100.0*

Note that the index weight has been calculated from the market capitalization for each stock divided by the market capitalization of the overall index. The fund manager's overall benchmark can be calculated at stock level as follows.

	Index Weight (%)	Benchmark Weight of Respective Market	Stock Level Benchmark Weight (%)
BT	12.5	60%	7.5
Glaxo	39.8	60%	23.9
Vodafone	47.7	60%	28.6
Ford	7.7	40%	3.1
Microsoft	44.3	40%	17.7
Texaco	6.0	40%	2.4
Wal-Mart	42.0	40%	16.8
Total	200.0		100.0

The fund manager now has a great deal more flexibility in how he can analyse his portfolio. For example, he can now compare his fund to the benchmark on a pan-global industrial sector basis by grouping the stocks in telecoms (here BT and Vodafone), pharmaceuticals etc together to create an implied industrial benchmark for his fund.

Indexing benchmark weights to reflect market movements since the benchmark was published

Many benchmarks based on peer group data are only published on a quarterly basis in arrears. This is due to the lead time required to gather the necessary data from each fund management house. In order to avoid running the fund against out of date benchmark data, fund managers will 'index-up' the published benchmark figures to reflect market movements since the publication of the peer group survey figures. Of course, this process will not take into account any changes in the asset allocations of the fund managers' rivals, but it will provide a better guide than unadjusted figures.

As an example, let us say that benchmark figures were published in September, that we are now in mid-October, and we want to calculate the current estimated benchmark. Given the following data.

	Benchmark Published Weight	Index Used	Index Start	Index End	% Change
UK Equities	54%	FTSE 100	6,000	6,600	10
Overseas Equities	21%	MSCI World ex-UK	2,500	2,250	−5
UK Bonds	12%	FTA Govt All Stocks	1,350	1,385	1
Overseas Bonds	7%	J P Morgan Govt ex-Sterling	4,500	4,050	−10
Cash	6%	3 Month LIBOR	110	112.2	2

the calculations would be carried out as follows.

	Benchmark Published Weight	Index % Change	Raw Indexed Benchmark	Adjusted Indexed Benchmark
UK Equities	54%	10	59.4%	57.2%
Overseas Equities	21%	−5	20.0%	19.2%
UK Bonds	12%	1	12.1%	11.7%
Overseas Bonds	7%	−10	6.3%	6.1%
Cash	6%	2	6.1%	5.9%
Total	*100%*		*103.9%*	*100.0%*

The adjustment is required since market movements will rarely cancel each other out.

CHAPTER 5

Asset Allocation

Introduction

The fund management company's overall investment strategy (often referred to as the 'house view') is generally periodically reviewed by senior investment directors in the light of current macroeconomic and market data and investment views shared across desks within the firm. The role of asset allocators is to decide on the proportions (or allocations) of clients' funds between equities, bonds, property and cash. In addition, asset allocation is also carried out within each broad market (ie between regions of the world for equities and across currency blocs and between government and corporate bonds for fixed interest). There is obviously a huge amount of information available to asset management houses, not the smallest source of which comes from brokerages falling over each other to flood the asset manager's doorstep with paper each morning. In general, however, the types of factors asset allocators are looking at include overall prospects for economic growth, interest rates, cost factors (eg wages, oil price etc), inflation prospects and business cycles.

Since the US remains the foremost global economic power and a huge importer of goods from many markets around the world, US economic indicators such as interest rates have significant implications for the rest of the world's economy. The relative strength of the US dollar is a connected, but slightly different, factor. Since US dollars are used so extensively, any increase in the value of the dollar will have an adverse effect on other currencies. Many emerging market economies are highly dependent upon the US for loans and other economic support, and will be highly sensitive to bad US economy news.

Political changes affect asset allocation in terms of prospective government's expected policy on government spending, interest rates, balance of payments strategy and economic management generally (particularly where this will affect inflation and currency strength).

Economic Data of Interest

As mentioned, the asset allocation process is driven by an array of economic data. These data influence the following four major factors: economic growth, inflation, interest rates and currency levels (however, it is important to note that these high level factors are interdependent; for example currency levels are dependent upon interest rates and economic growth prospects). In general, forecasted changes regarding these four major factors will have the following implications for asset allocators.

Scenario	*Forecasted Changes*	*Possible Impact on Markets*
Economic Growth	Increased Pace	▶ Strong equity growth in short term ▶ Increased inflation risk – longer bonds depressed
Inflation	Increase	▶ 'Inflation-proofing' of equities attractive; *however*, equity earnings value eroded in longer term ▶ Bonds generally down due to lower real cash flow values, especially at long end ▶ Index-linked bonds more attractive
Interest Rates	Increase	▶ Equities down through effect on earnings NPVs ▶ Bonds down through cash flow NPV reduction ▶ Cash/ Short bond allocation attractive since higher rates available

Scenario	Forecasted Changes	Possible Impact on Markets
Currency Levels	Increase	▷ All asset classes increase in value for non-domiciled holders ▷ Equity earnings affected by: ▷ Fall in demand abroad since goods more expensive ▷ Cheaper import competitiont. Bond markets strengthen due to anticipated interest rate increase

Other factors include government fiscal policy, such as money supply changes which can lead to expectations of inflation increases, which may in turn lead to interest rate rises to 'damp down' inflationary pressures. In addition, there is a degree of interdependence between markets; eg a general rise in bond yields will tend to increase the currency of denomination, as well as reducing the amount of funding sourced from bond issuance in favour of equity.

The data used in asset allocation, along with some suggested asset allocation actions, include the following.

Economic Growth

Indicator	Expected/ Forecast Status	Possible Asset Allocation Action
Economic Cycle Stage	Upswing/boom	High allocation to equities (for growth)
	Heading for 'Soft Landing'	Higher allocation to equities
	Heading for 'Hard Landing'	Higher allocation to bonds/cash
	Recession	Low allocation to equities

Indicator	*Expected/ Forecast Status*	*Possible Asset Allocation Action*
Interest Rates	Increasing	Higher cash allocation
		Higher allocation to quality bonds
	Decrease	Higher bond and equity allocation
Government Spending	Increase	Higher allocation to equities (demand increase)
		Lower allocation to bonds (especially corporates) due to probable PSBR rise:
		— Higher supply of government reduces price
		— Crowding out of public sector borrowers[12]
Consumer Spending	Increase	Higher allocation to equities

Inflation

Productivity	Increase	Higher allocation to equities (lower unit costs)
Wage Levels	Increase	Reduce allocation to equities
		Reduce allocation to bonds
	Decrease	Increase allocation to equities
		Increase allocation to bonds
Oil Price	Increase	Lower allocation to oil dependent equities[13]
		Lower allocation to bonds (inflation effect)

[12] Greater supply of bonds decreases prices (increasing yields, making it more expensive for corporates to borrow).
[13] Since the oil crisis of the 1970s oil consumption as a percentage of Gross Domestic Product (GDP) has decreased significantly for most developed nations. Investment strategists are latterly taking the view that oil prices will affect specific companies' earnings more than government economic policies.

Indicator	Expected/ Forecast Status	Possible Asset Allocation Action
Government Spending	Increase	Lower allocation to bonds
House Prices	Increase	Higher allocation to property

Interest Rates

Central Bank Base Rate	Increase	Increase cash allocation
Corporate Bond Spreads	Widening	Reduce allocation to corporates

Currency Levels

Other Currency Strength	Increase	Increase equity allocation (increased overseas demand), focus on exporters to that market. Hedge currency
Currency Level	Increase	Decrease equity allocation Domestic equities suffer from lower demand Overseas equities worth less Consider hedging foreign positions
Current Account Deficit	Increase	Increase equity allocation ahead of currency devaluation

Market Specific Asset Allocation Considerations

Equities

The following is a high level summary of the factors affecting general allocation to equities.

Cost Factors Impacting Earnings

Interest rate prospects are of concern, especially with recent governments' standard interest rate increase responses to inflationary pressures. Companies will suffer higher funding costs accompanied by higher wage claims. Additionally, as mentioned above, domestic interest rate rises also increase the domestic currency's strength, reducing export demand. This factor is becoming increasingly important with the growing internationalization of companies (eg Vodafone which derives over 60% of its earnings from outside its country of domicile).

Other significant factors that affect different industrial sectors in different ways include the oil price, wage inflation, productivity and threats to certain markets through the instigation or removal of trade barriers.

Inter-relationship with corporate bond market

Most corporates are borrowers as well as issuers of equity, and are seeking to gain a greater return on new projects in their industry than that paid in terms of borrowing costs. There are a few exceptions, the so-called 'cash rich' corporates, historical examples being GEC and BT, who are less interest rate sensitive since they can finance projects out of their own funds. However, in general expected interest rate rises are bad news for equities.

Stockmarket Factors

Like any market, the price of equities is partially driven by the demand and supply for the equity investment vehicles themselves. Examples of market demand and supply factors have included the end of the US mutual fund tax year and the 'January effect'[14].

The Technology Factor

Technological advance is a modern day 'backdrop' factor carefully monitored by asset managers. Technological innovation has had an unequal effect on different industries. As an example, a comparison of retailers with telecoms companies in the UK between the end of 1987 and the end of 2000 shows that technology has hugely increased the percentage of the market that telecoms represent. The main impact of this

---

[14] Empirical evidence suggests that demand for equities increases in January, normally accompanied by an increase in prices.

is that factors affecting technology based companies (such as the price of microprocessing chips) will have an increasing effect on the market as a whole.

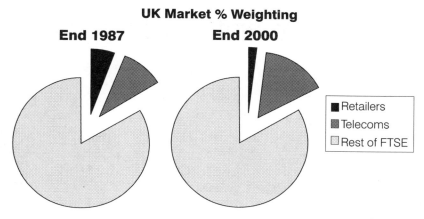

Source: Datastream

CHAPTER 6

Instrument Overview

Whilst the following gives an overview of the investible universe available to the fund manager, it is important to emphasize that most pension fund, life fund and unitized vehicle fund management is carried out by investing in mainstream, liquid securities. Investment in more exotic, risky and illiquid instruments is left to specialist fund managers, or those not subject to the stringent rules imposed by such regulators as the UK's Financial Services Authority (FSA).

Equities

The main attractive feature of equities is their well-established track record of growth, particularly since the 1939–45 war. Investors are prepared to take more risk than before in order to enjoy the benefits of the growth seen in equities in recent years, and have been increasingly prepared to forgo income in the form of dividends in order to enjoy capital growth of their equity holdings.

Unlike bonds and cash, equities can provide spectacular price appreciation. However, they are also more volatile and equity holders stand to lose all of their original investment (this has actually happened, even in the UK, eg Polly Peck). However, it is fairly well accepted that, in the longer term, equities have represented the 'best'[15] investment vehicle, and an effective hedge for the investor against the ravages of inflation. Price appreciation generally occurs due to a positive change in the prospects for a given firm. This could be due to a piece of macro-economic news such as the fall in price of one of the firm's major cost factors (eg oil or labour). Otherwise it could be industry specific, such as a change in legislation opening up new markets to firms in that industry. It could also be due to more firm-specific news such as successful selling into a new market, or innovation giving that firm a competitive edge against its rivals.

[15] 'Best' means a higher risk adjusted return, which will be covered in detail later.

In the event of default, equity holders are 'junior' to bondholders; ie any remaining assets will be distributed to debtholders first. Since equity holders are the owners of the company (rather than lenders) the quid pro quo for enjoying the benefits of upside prosperity is that they lose out completely in the event of the company going into liquidation[16]. Most equities also provide investors with a source of income, this being paid in the form of dividends. In latter years this element of an equity's return has become less important. In particular high-tech firms that need to retain their cash in order to invest in research and development for new products etc have tended not to pay dividends (Microsoft have successfully adopted this strategy).

In modern times, nearly all equity is issued in Ordinary Share form. Other forms of equity such as Preference Shares are becoming increasingly rare, perhaps due to the growth of the Eurobond market. New issues of shares sometimes allow investors to spread the cost of their outlay over a period of time. In this situation the equity will migrate through stages of being Nil Paid (where the investor has been allocated the stock, but not paid for it), Partly Paid through to Fully Paid. All of these stages will be separate investment entities, each with its own market price. Initial Public Offerings (IPOs) and Private Placements are essentially the same as new issues; the only real difference is that IPOs must be made available to the investing public, whereas Private Placements are offered to specific investors by the broker managing the issue.

There are specific difficulties with Emerging Market equities, ie equity issued in countries such as Mexico, India and within Eastern Europe. One issue is availability; due to the small market capitalization it may be difficult to track down required shares. Another is that investments may not be removable from the country of domicile. Lastly such markets often have absurdly long (by developed markets' standards) settlement periods. In order to circumvent these problems, fund managers often use 'depository receipts'. These are securities issued by brokers which are backed by the broker's own holdings of the underlying securities. The price of the depository receipt will be higher than the underlying security, to compensate the broker for the service thus provided (ie holding share

---

[16] In reality, however, companies with any serious chance of going bust will find it very difficult to borrow capital on a debt issuance basis.

certificates in its offices within the equity's country of domicile). However, this is generally viewed as a worthwhile premium to pay, given the improved liquidity, removal of current or potential capital withdrawal restrictions and relative ease of settlement. Depository receipts are generally issued as ADRs (American Depository Receipts issued in the US), GDRs (Global Depository Receipts issued in Luxembourg or IDRs (International Depository Receipts issued in any financial centre).

Bonds

Fixed interest instruments' chief feature is that they offer a constant, predictable source of return in the form of a coupon (or a discount in the case of zero coupon bonds). The implication of this for fund managers is that they can predict, with a fairly high level of certainty, the return that they will obtain. This represents a significant difference from equities, where the bulk of returns in modern times is derived from capital appreciation of the stock price. Having said this, the price of bonds can fall, leading to a reduction in the overall 'holding period return' of the bond (unless the bond is held to maturity). The reasons for a fall in the price of bonds include a general rise in interest rates, an increase in supply or similar bonds (eg the recent oversupply of telecoms industry debt) and changes in the creditworthiness of issuers. The behaviour of bonds is analysed in further detail in the Fixed Interest Management chapter.

Bond portfolios' market exposures are broadly broken down by analysts according to type of issuer and currency of denomination. An example of a simple fund analysis showing the fund manager his weighted duration exposure in each market segment might be as follows.

Currency of Denomination

Type of Issuer	US Dollar	Sterling	Yen	Euro
Government	2.1	1.1	0.9	0.6
Government Emerging	0.8			
Corporate Investment Grade	1.3	0.6	0.2	0.2
Corporate High Yield	0.5	0.1		

Thus the overall duration of the portfolio (of 8.4 years) gives a measure of the overall market risk, whilst the figures for each segment give a measure of the risk allocated to that part of the market. These figures are, in fact, much more useful when compared to the portfolio's benchmark (this is covered in more detail later).

For all bonds, the time to maturity is an important metric since it provides a measure of the market risk of the bond. Corporate bonds are also heavily influenced by credit ratings, which provide a measure of the risk of default of a bond.

Many bonds have special features (rather than being 'plain vanilla'). These features are included for the following reasons. One is to make the bond more attractive to potential investors by offering such features as an option to convert the bond into equity in the company issuing the bond (a 'convertible') or the ability to sell the bond back to the issuer at a specified price (a 'puttable' bond). Another reason is to reduce the issuer's risk, for example by the existence of a paydown schedule, where the issuer repays some of the debt early (a 'sinking fund') or an option to buy back the bond from the investor at an agreed price (a 'callable' bond). Lastly, some features exist in order to fit in with the collateral base of the issue. Where a bond is backed by an asset such as mortgages that are periodically repaid, the bond will implicitly contain a 'sinking fund' option. The difference from the previous example is that the paydown schedule will not be known since it will depend on the propensity of homeowners to repay capital on their mortgages over the life of the bond.

Money Market

Money market, or 'cash' instruments are used to invest clients' funds for short periods of time. Cash is used as a defensive asset class, since its guaranteed (but lower) interest rate and shorter time to maturity make it a low risk option. Another reason for moving into cash might be that the fund manager wants to take profits out of equities and/or bonds. By selling equities and moving the funds into cash, he will be able to move back into equities when the market has fallen back to (in his view) the correct level, thereby making a profit for the fund. Cash instruments are also used to invest cash that is available for a short period of time (eg from the receipt of a coupon until the coupon is reinvested in the bond market).

The types of instruments available to fund managers include the following.

Instrument	Features
Call Deposits	Funds deposited for an agreed number of days at an agreed interest rate
US Government Treasury Bills (T-Bills)	Short dated paper issued by the US Government, usually between one month and one year
Floating Rate Notes (FRNs)	Short dated paper (eg 3 month maturity). Interest rate 'floats' above a reference rate such as 3 month LIBOR making it a low interest rate risk option
Repurchase Agreements (Repos)	Basically a collateralized loan, the collateral usually being a high quality, liquid bond (eg US Treasury). The trade is set up so that the bond is sold and then repurchased. The key is that the lender is in possession of the bond in the event of default on behalf of the borrower
Instrument	*Features*
Short Term Income Funds (STIFs)	Funds set up specifically to invest in money market instruments. The advantage to the fund manager of investing in units of these funds (rather than directly in cash instruments) is increased diversification of risk across issuers/maturities and ease of administration

Property

Property fund managers generally favour commercial property since the costs of administration are lower. Property funds are usually managed by a specialist team or separate company set up to manage rent admin-istration, lease contracts etc. Asset allocators tend to invest in units of funds run by specialists.

Derivatives

Asset managers are generally very restricted in their use of derivatives, despite their potential for reducing fund risk, and their usefulness in giving immediate exposure to any given market.

Futures are sometimes used to hedge a fund manager's position in a given market. They can be very useful for short-term reductions in a fund manager's exposure to a market, since he can take a single short futures position which he subsequently reverses, rather than having to sell and then buy back a large number of equities. For very large funds this is potentially a very useful device, since it is difficult for fund managers to move large quantities of equities without adversely affecting their prices. Additionally, futures are used to expedite asset allocation switches. Thus if a fund manager wishes to move from UK equities into Japanese equities, he could immediately sell a LIFFE FTSE 100 future and buy a TSE Nikkei 225 future giving him an immediate exposure change. He can then use the time that this has bought him to 'unwind the future to physical', selling UK equities currently out of favour and buying Japanese equities with good prospects at favourable prices.

Options are infrequently used in mainstream fund management, due to the extremely risky reputation that they have acquired.

Forward foreign exchange (FX) contracts are commonly used to change a fund's currency exposure, whilst leaving assets invested in underlying markets. Their use is described in the Currency Management chapter.

Interest rate swaps are agreements to exchange series of fixed rate cash flows (eg from a fixed interest fund) for a rate that 'floats' above a reference rate (eg 3 month LIBOR). They can, therefore, provide an excellent hedge against adverse interest rate changes for fixed interest fund managers. Another advantage is that the swap market is extremely liquid, making it easy for agreements to be tailored to the fund manager's exact requirements.

CHAPTER 7

Equity Fund Management

Introduction

Equity fund management is often viewed as an easy option; in the long run equities have generally delivered exceptional returns, outstripping other forms of investment in most long term periods (eg ten years plus).

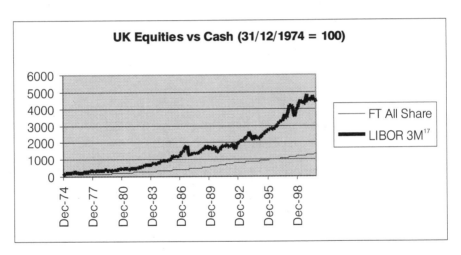

UK Equities vs Cash (31/12/1974 = 100)

The reality of equity fund management is somewhat different, however. The market is highly competitive, with an increasingly knowledgeable, demanding and sophisticated client base. Equity fund managers' returns are constantly compared to other types of investment and to other fund managers. League tables are published in most quality Sunday newspapers, and fund managers' approaches and performances are themselves analysed with their ratings being made available to the investing public[18].

[17] London Interbank Offered Rate (13 months).
[18] An example is Fund Research, which analyses fund managers' perfomance using risk/return measures and rates most fund managers in the market according to these measures with an AAA, AA etc style rating.

In addition, equity managers are often constrained in terms of which securities they can buy, since they need reliable data for a reasonably long period to enable them to make sensible comparisons. Thus, few mainstream fund managers would have included *lastminute.com* in their portfolios (even if they had wished to) since little or no analytical data was available for a reasonable time period.

There are many sources of return and risk on equity portfolios. They include, but are by no means limited to:

▶ Country

▶ Industry Group (Energy, Financials, Technology)

▶ Economic 'Theme' (eg Consumer Cyclicals, Defensive, Interest Rate Sensitive etc)

▶ Beta (ie weighted average beta giving a measure of overall portfolio risk)

▶ Company Size (based on Market Capitalization)

Since these risks are not all hierarchical see below.

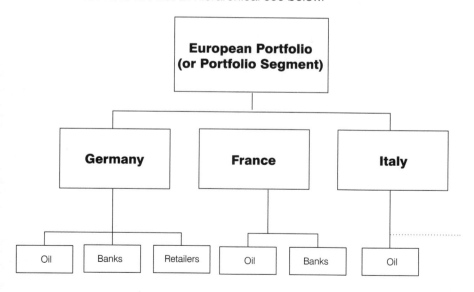

but often orthogonal (ie overlapping, so for example, a security might be a medium size, Consumer Cyclical, low beta stock), the fund manager must constantly consider his portfolio's positions from a number of perspectives using a number of different reports, preferably showing his position relative to his benchmark.

This chapter looks at the objectives of an equity fund manager, ie what he needs to deliver, and then moves on to the types of research and analysis that fund managers carry out in order to allocate client funds across sectors and invest in individual securities.

Objectives

Maximizing returns

Equity fund managers are broadly divided into two types, firstly those seeking to achieve the highest possible capital return (ie increasing the value of the fund as much as possible) given the 'charter' of the fund. This 'charter' specifies the market(s) and the universe of securities in which it can invest (eg quoted/unquoted). The other type of manager is looking to provide an element of income for investors, whilst protecting the client's capital base (as far as possible) from the ravages of inflation. In practice, there is little difference in the way analysis is carried out for each, since it does not really matter whether dividends are paid out or retained. The difference will come in terms of the actual stocks picked by the fund manager when constructing his portfolio from the list of preferred stocks (ie those with good prospects) prepared by the asset management house's analysts. A growth fund manager will be looking to include stocks with the maximum potential for capital appreciation within a given time horizon, whereas the income fund manager will be constrained to include stocks with a relatively high dividend yield in order to achieve the cash flows required for investors.

Both types of manager will be judged against a benchmark. The measure of a successful fund manager is to *consistently* beat their peer-group benchmark. To achieve consistency, the equity fund manager and his research assistants must initially identify, and then build diversified portfolios from, stocks that will outperform other stocks in the indices that constitute the peer-group benchmark. Before moving onto an examination of the techniques used by equity fund managers, let us first look at the sources of return from an equity.

Price Appreciation

The main source of return from equities is derived from increases in the market price. Like any investment, the price of an equity should be equal to the net present value (NPV) of the cash flows received in the future by the investor. Although this model still holds for equities, it is seen as a longer term relationship. In the short term, equity prices are often strongly influenced by prevailing general stock market conditions (eg sentiment, liquidity, seasonal factors such as the January effect, hype etc). The long-term relationship holds the key to whether an equity is currently over- or underpriced, and is generally analysed by looking at the earnings of a company. These earnings may or may not be paid out to the investor in the form of dividends, but nonetheless provide the basis of the fundamental value of an equity. Like any net present value analysis, one of the key factors relates to interest rate expectations; ie if interest rates are expected to rise, then the NPV will fall. If earnings are retained, the company can use them to grow the business, assuming that it has a sufficient number of new projects in which it can achieve a worthwhile return (eg the development of a new project). If we compare the 1988 to 1992 performance of ICI, which traditionally paid a high dividend, to Microsoft, which re-invested corporate earnings in research and development for new products etc, we can see that the Microsoft investor would have benefited hugely from this policy.

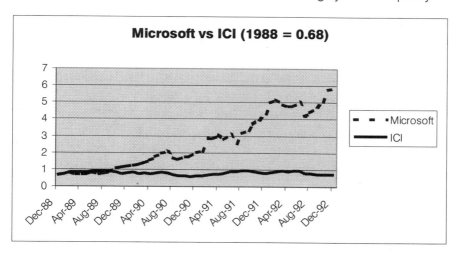

Dividends

Dividends are payments made to investors, representing a portion of the firm's earnings. If earnings are paid out in the form of dividends, and the fund manager does not need them to meet his clients' income needs, then he has the problem of reinvesting them to achieve the same rate of return. In addition, the fund may be subject to income tax. It is for these reasons, and due to the increasing requirement for investment in technology, that there is an increasing trend towards the non-payment of dividends.

Other Sources of Equity Returns

Equity holders can also benefit from rights issues, which are essentially offers by the company in which they are invested to purchase further shares at a price below the current market price. This saves the company the expense and effort of raising funds in the open market, and gives the fund manager the potential to enjoy an additional return from the difference between the rights price and the market price. Similarly, equity holders can receive scrips which are 'free' shares issued to them, often in the place of a dividend. Receiving stock in this way can have tax advantages; however, it is not necessarily the case that the fund manager will be better off, since the scrip issue is essentially diluting the issued share capital of the equity. These events are usually referred to as 'corporate actions', the administration for which is usually carried out by the fund manager's 'back office'.

Given their large capital base, fund managers are often involved in underwriting new issues of shares. Here the fund manager will guarantee the purchase of a tranche of shares from the investment bank arranging the issue, in the (usually unlikely) event that the shares are not taken up. In the US equity market Initial Public Offerings (IPOs) have become popular. These are companies being floated on the market for the first time by a broker or investment bank. Generally these shares are sold to asset managers ahead of a full launch at a price lower than their anticipated real value, the idea being to avoid the cost of an underwriting fee. The US Securities and Exchange Commission (SEC) have very strict rules regarding the types of fund that can invest in IPOs. The key is that, since they are issued on the basis that they are for the 'public', they can only be purchased by funds that, themselves, are generally available to the public, ie whose units can easily be bought and sold by anyone.

Security and Market Analysis

General

Fund managers and their analysts have a large amount of data at their disposal, ranging from economic data affecting the prospects for equities generally to stock specific data giving an insight into the prospects for, and the riskiness of, particular equities. Information is available on a time-series basis, enabling analysts to identify trends such as the increased profitability, growth etc of the company. There are several measures used by analysts, usually expressed as a ratio enabling comparisons between companies. The main ratios are as follows.

PE Ratio	*Price divided by earnings per share, discussed in detail below*
Gearing	The ratio of debt to equity financing. A high proportion of debt financing can potentially lead to greater share price volatility since the firm will have a higher sensitivity to interest rate changes
Dividend Cover	A measure of the safety margin that a firm has in being able to pay its expected dividend
Price to Cash Flow	Important since cash flow problems are a significant source of corporate distress
Return on Capital Employed	Can be used to compare the performance of directors in utilizing a firm's capital with alternative investments
Price to Net Asset Value	Can be viewed as a measure of the goodwill or brand value of a company, or of its overpricing by the equity market

The source of this data is generally published company accounts. Analysts need to be very careful in their use of the data, since they must take into account the basis used for items such as depreciation etc in order that they can make a fair comparison between firms. It is particularly important to understand the accounting conventions and reporting requirements for overseas companies. In many cases conventions will differ (eg Last In, First Out (LIFO) versus First In, First Out etc) and regulatory requirements for company account reporting may not be as stringent as in the UK.

Comparing Equities

Whether interested in deriving good returns from cash flows (in the form of dividend income) or stock price appreciation (through company growth), a major input to an equity analyst's security selection process will be corporate earnings, which is the post-tax profit for the period (usually one financial year). These earnings are derived from the company's profit and loss account as follows:

Sales Revenue – Cost of Sales = Gross Profit

Gross Profit – Distribution Costs – Administration Costs = Trading Profit

Trading Profit + Other Income – Interest Payable = Pre-Tax Profit

Pre-Tax Profit – Tax Payable = Post-Tax Profit

This type of breakdown is useful for analysts, since they can more accurately attribute changes in the stock price. For example, if an oil firm's earnings fall due to a temporary fall in the barrel price of oil, an analyst may be less concerned than if administration costs show a long term upward trend, suggesting management inefficiency.

The theory behind this significance of earnings when comparing equities is very simply that any security's price must represent the net present value (NPV) of cash flows expected from it. A simple model, looking at a three year investment horizon, might be as follows:

$$\text{Current\_Price} = \frac{\text{Div}_{\text{Year1}}}{1+r} + \frac{\text{Div}_{\text{Year2}}}{(1+r)^2} + \frac{\text{Div}_{\text{Year3}}}{(1+3)^3} + \frac{\text{MarketPrice}_{\text{Year3}}}{(1+r)^3}$$

The simplifying assumptions here are that:

1. All earnings are paid out as dividends

2. There is no growth in the earnings (here the same as the dividend)

3. Interest rates remain constant through the entire investment horizon

Even in this simple, and rather unrealistic, model there is still an unknown variable, namely the actual value of the market price of the security in three years' time. In the real world any assumptions would be subject to subjective judgement and fluctuation. The proportion of earnings paid out in the form of dividends (referred to as the dividend payout ratio) can fluctuate through time as the firm's directors decide whether to pay dividends to shareholders, or to retain the earnings for investment in new projects. Earnings growth is the norm, and the subject of in-depth analysis by both brokers' and equity fund managers' analysts. Interest rates, which will clearly affect the NPV of projected earnings, are also liable to fluctuation and are therefore the subject of forecasting by economic analysts.

Given this importance of earnings to the price of a security, they are the subject of detailed study by analysts, who will prepare estimates of corporate earnings going out several years into the future. From this they will calculate the earnings per share (EPS) ratio from these earnings estimates divided by the number of shares in issue. This will then enable them to calculate one of the main comparative metrics for equities, the Price/Earnings (P/E) ratio (simply from the current market price divided by the earnings per share estimate).

Another method of comparing equities is by looking at the value of the assets that the company owns, the metric here being the net asset value. This is important for companies with lower growth prospects than high-tech businesses such as telecoms.

Types of Securities

In recent years industrial growth has been increasingly influenced by technological advance, particularly in the field of computerization. In addition to information technology industries themselves (eg semi-conductor production, software houses etc), telecommunication companies (eg mobile phones, digital networking etc) are highly sensitive to innovation as well as costs of production factors[19]. Thus newer

[19] Interestingly microchips are now traded on a commodity basis like gold, pork bellies and greasy wool. This enables companies for whom chips represent a significant cost to manage their risk by buying chips forward, thereby 'locking in' an agreed price in the future extremely high.

industries such as technology and telecoms have a greater emphasis on company growth potential as well as (international) competitive threats and regulatory issues. One feature of new technology-led industries is low barriers to entry, particularly in the Internet world[20], making constant investment in research and development to stay ahead of the existing and potential competition vital. In other industries, such as gas marketing, privatization and deregulation has allowed new players to enter the market.

Although affected to a degree by technological advance, older industries are not expected to grow at such phenomenal rates. They also have higher barriers to entry (plant building and set up costs etc). For these reasons more emphasis is placed on traditional analyses such as the impact of projected interest rate changes on earnings, costs of factors of production and longer-term industry longevity factors (eg the demise of facsimile machines given the advent of electronic mail).

The implication of these factors is that, when analysing securities, it is essential to take account of the industry group to which any stock belongs. Thus when carrying out fundamental analysis[21], comparing securities from different industries is fraught with difficulties. This can be explained by considering equity prices to be derived from the following function:

$$\text{Price} = F(\text{Earnings}, \text{Growth}_{\text{Earnings}}, \text{Certainty}_{\text{Earnings}}, \text{Interest\_Rates})$$

This function highlights the key differential between stocks in established industries and newer, more technology driven industries using the earnings growth metric. Earnings growth will generally be expected to be much higher for newer industries, whereas more established industries will offer a higher earnings certainty factor. Thus comparison between equities in different industry groups is difficult.

This function also provides an insight into the reason why fund managers tend to avoid new companies such as *lastminute.com*. Although the projected earnings figures published may look attractive, the certainty factor will be considerably lower than for other, more established companies in the equity market.

---

[20] Although, as we have seen, the on-going costs of publicity, measured in terms of cost per 'hit' can be extremely high. However, this does not prevent initial start-up.

[21] Fundamental analysis of equities is used to describe the interpretation of company accounts data in order to assess the accuracy of a particular equity's current market price.

News: What Data Is Important?

In order to outperform the benchmark, fund managers need to gather, interpret and act upon market information generally available to all market participants. According to the Efficient Market Hypothesis (EMH) all existing information is already priced into securities, making new information 'news'. This news would include the following types.

Type of News	Example of News Category	Impact
Macro-Economic	GDP	General growth trend of economy, indicator of whether demand will increase or decrease
	Inflation	Increases costs, reduces real value of future earnings
	Interest Rates	Affects discounting of earnings, increases cost of borrowing
Equity Market Specific	Influx/Outflow of Capital	Increases/decreases prices through change in demand
	Over-Buying/Panic Selling	Inflates/Deflates market compared to fundamentals
Industry Specific	Innovation	Reduces attractiveness of existing firms in an industry
	Factor Costs	Reduces earnings potential
Stock Specific	Interim/Full Results	Positive if better than expected

Managing Risk

Equities are notoriously volatile investments, despite their well established long term inflation proofing and high capital growth record. Fund managers have to be extremely disciplined and level headed when considering which securities to buy and sell, having faith in their own selection methodologies rather than being carried away on a wave of market hype. Fund managers will ask the following types of question when considering whether securities should be included in their portfolios:

Data availability – is data available over a sufficient time period to establish a firm's 'track record'?

Cash flow analysis – a major cause of problems for large and small firms alike. An example is the recent difficulties experienced by telecoms companies competing with each other to fund expansion and R&D

Beta – is the company particularly sensitive to overall market movements? The fund manager may seek to control exposure by keeping the weighted beta of the market within certain guidelines

Gearing – If a company is highly geared, ie it has a high proportion of debt capital relative to equity capital, its earnings will be more volatile, since the firm will be committed to paying fixed interest payments whether sales revenues are forthcoming or not

Interpreting the Data: Equity Management 'Styles'

Equity fund managers are generally divided into two camps with regard to their analysis approach. They are generally categorized as 'Value' managers and 'Growth' managers. Depending on their approach, analysts will differ in their interpretation of one of the main ratios used, the P/E ratio. If a P/E ratio is 'high' (either relative to other equities in the sector, or relative to its own previous levels) it would generally be viewed by value managers as being unattractive. Growth managers would probably take a different view, perhaps seeing the high P/E ratio as an indicator that the market views the security as having good growth prospects. The growth manager would decide whether he felt that the company's growth prospects are correctly priced by the market, before deciding to buy or sell.

Summarizing the key data items used by growth managers and the three generally recognized types of value managers, along with their interpretation of the data.

Type of Manager	Key Data Items	Interpretation
Growth	P/E Ratio	High P/E ratio may indicate good growth prospects
Value – Low P/E	P/E Ratio	Low P/E ratio indicates low price relative to future earnings
Value – Contrarian	Price to Book	May have low earnings, but could benefit from a firm specific reversal of fortune
Value – High Yield	Dividend Yield	High ratio of dividend over price indicates good value, since represents a relatively high return on capital invested

Asset management companies tend to have specialist teams looking at smaller capitalization ('small cap') stocks. This is mainly because security level data is not available from the usual market data providers (eg Bloomberg, Datastream etc) as it is for larger equities. Additionally, it is less relevant to analyse smaller companies according to their industry group (although it is still one factor for consideration). The key to small cap management is to gather as much information about each company under consideration, either from brokers specializing in the company and/or from the company itself.

Trading

Fund managers generally take a long-term view on markets, corresponding to the general role of their funds as a longer term investment vehicle for their clients. However, they will 'switch' out of equities that they view as expensive (using their own measure) into stocks that they view as 'cheap' (ie they expect these securities to appreciate). By doing this they expect to make a profit for the fund, whilst retaining the 'shape' of the fund, ie its relative exposures to different industry groups etc. Other factors making stocks attractive in the shorter term are the likelihood of a takeover bid, which generally results in a market price rise, and expected (short term) changes in fashion and taste.

Portfolio Construction

General

The methodology used by fund managers to construct their portfolios will very much depend on the type of fund that they are managing, as well as the style of management that they use. Although there are many general funds, such as segregated pension funds, that invest globally, there is a continuing trend towards specialization in particular markets. Each market will have its own principal considerations, a summary of which is given below.

Market Specialization	*Considerations/Approach*
Global	Global market allocation
UK	Industry allocation
Continental European	– Allocation between Euro-in/Euro-out – Allocation across markets – Allocation to European Emerging
Japan	– Financial/Non-Financial Allocation – Industry allocation
Asia Pacific Ex-Japan	– Allocation across markets
Market Specialization	*Considerations/Approach*
Latin America	– Market allocation – Stock specific analysis
Emerging Markets	– Market allocation – Stock specific analysis
Smaller Companies	Stock specific selection

Thus equity management involves an element of asset allocation, either to countries managed by the European, Far Eastern, Latin American or Emerging Markets desks, or to industries within single countries, especially within the UK. Having said this, the internationalization of many companies in recent years has resulted in fund managers looking at industry grouping irrespective of the country in which the corporate is based. Since firms derive an increasing proportion of their earnings from countries outside their domicile, it is becoming less and less relevant to analyse them on the basis of economic prospects for that country (eg GDP growth etc). More relevant are the issues facing each industry (see below for a comparison of the telecoms and oil sectors). Glaxo Wellcome have traditionally derived the greatest proportion (over 40%) of their earnings from overseas. Others, such as Vodafone, are rapidly increasing the percentages earned outside the UK.

Vodafone: Source of Earnings

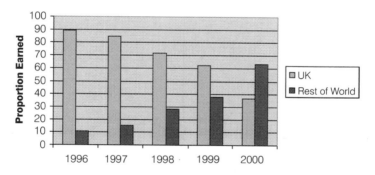

Source: Datastream

The number of different influences on a portfolio are quite diverse. This creates the need for a broad range of different analyses so that the fund manager can look at his portfolio broken down in different ways. Particularly useful are analyses of portfolios giving the weights allocated to each category, especially where these weights are compared to the constituents of the index used as part or all of the fund's benchmark.

Other Analyses

Equities are sensitive to a number of different factors affecting their market prices in the short, medium or long term. This means that the fund manager needs to look at his portfolio, and the securities held in them, from a number of different perspectives and involves assimilating the huge quantities of data available to fund managers, sourced from external brokers as well as their own firms' analysts. The key is the interpretation of the data; what does the news imply for a security or overall industry grouping?

Portfolio level analyses include the following.

Fund breakdown by:

Company size –   in an economic upswing smaller companies may grow faster than larger firms, whilst in a recession investors may prefer larger, more resilient (through cash availability or diversification) companies

Economic theme –   eg sensitivities to oil price, interest rates, factors affecting other economies into which products are sold[22]

Overall portfolio factors such as the fund's beta can also provide useful risk information. As with most types of fund level analysis, the comparison of the fund against the benchmark is the most useful.

Other security level analyses include the price to earnings ratio growth which is a dynamic measure of a trend of changing value (if you are a value-style manager) or changing growth (if you are a growth manager). If it is important to the fund manager that he receives dividends (eg if he is running an income fund), then he might look at the 'dividend cover', which is the ratio of earnings per share over dividends per share (ie a measure of how easily a company can afford to pay the dividend). Again, the trend of this over time will be useful information.

Industry Case Studies

Each industrial sector will be affected differently by macroeconomic news as well as by industry specific factors, such as technological innovation. The following is a very high level review of three industrial sectors, included in an attempt to bring out the fact that industries need to be individually analysed by fund managers.

[22] A dramatic example was the New Zealand economy, which went into recession in the early 1970s after the UK (its principal importer) joined the European Common Market.

Telecoms

The telecommunications industry is a relatively new sector and is still experiencing a high rate of growth as its market continues to develop. Let us look at the share prices for two participants, Vodafone and British Telecom, for the period from 1 January 1989 to 1 January 2001, displayed as relative to the FT All Share. While BT's relative growth over this period is impressive (590% to the FT All Share's 350%), it is somewhat eclipsed by the performance of Vodafone at 2,500% growth.

However, the threats to the industry and consequent risks to market value are severe. In recent months several factors have had a detrimental effect on the sector. These include the high level of market competition (assisted by deregulation, internationalization and general removal of barriers to entry). In addition, on-going research and development costs and huge third generation data (3G) licence fees have given rise to a huge requirement and consequent competition for funding (making borrowing in the bond markets both difficult to achieve and expensive). From 1 January 2000 to 1 January 2001, the industry has struggled.

In addition to these general issues, distinctive sub-themes are emerging within the industry. One of these is the type of service delivery platform used, the themes broadly being 'cable' or 'satellite' delivery. Since subscribers will generally choose one delivery mechanism or another, and will subsequently be relatively difficult to prise away, the key is to capture market share. Interestingly, the satellite camp (eg BSkyB) have stolen a march on the cable suppliers (eg Telewest), despite the fact that their technology base is relatively inelegant.

Thus this sub-theme can be seen to be a very important factor; both firms performed well initially, on the back of the general Telecoms boom, but BSkyB are now in the ascendancy further to their 'first mover' advantage in bringing their digital product to market. This analysis also emphasizes the importance of all aspects of a business (eg effective marketing as well as innovation and development capabilities).

Oil

The oil industry is a relatively old (especially compared to telecoms), well-established industry. The oligopolistic market structure is unlikely to

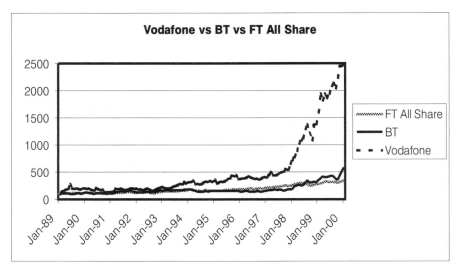

Source: Datastream

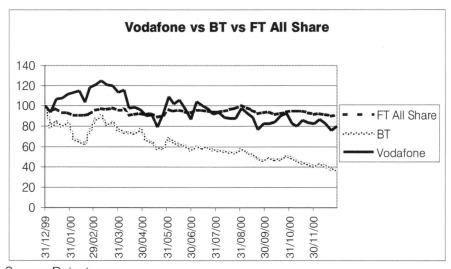

Source: Datastream

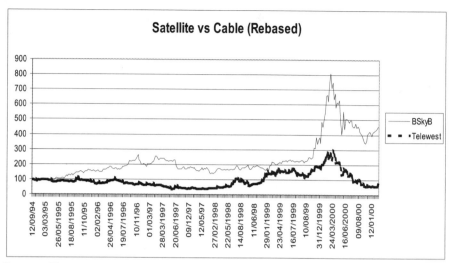

Source: Datastream

change significantly in the foreseeable future. Other features of the market include the setting of the underlying commodity price by the Organization of Petroleum Exporting Countries (OPEC) which is dominated by Saudi Arabia. The market has a very low elasticity of demand, but this is tempered by the existence of effective political and public pressure (eg where Esso were forced to renounce a price increase announced by its chairman in October 2000 after a public outcry).

In general, stocks are likely to move in line with each other, since they will be affected by the same factors roughly equally, one of the principal factors obviously being the prevailing commodity market barrel price of oil.

Consumer Goods

The consumer goods sector is strongly affected by macroeconomic factors, as well as changes in tastes which will affect the sales revenue and profits of individual firms. One of the key assets for consumer goods firms is the strength of their brand. A good example of this can be seen with companies such as Marks and Spencer and Next, which have seen their company valuation wax and wane on the basis of, *inter alia*, the strength of their brand.

Macroeconomic factors having a significant impact on consumer goods firms include the following. Rises in the expected costs of production, particularly labour, which represents a very high proportion of the cost of goods, will have a detrimental effect on this sector. Demand factors, which might include the savings ratio, will affect firms' 'pricing power', ie their ability to determine retail prices. Similarly the strengthening of the exchange rate between the firm's currency of domicile and that of its major export markets will reduce the competitiveness of goods and tend to reduce sales revenue, profits and consequently equity earnings.

Specialist Fund Types

The vast majority of funds fall into a very standard general management approach. Benchmark outperformance is sought through utilizing top-down asset allocation (which has been shown to generate a large proportion of a fund's returns) accompanied by the holding of securities, within each category, which represent good 'value', or have relatively high 'growth' prospects according to the fund manager's selection systems.

The main departures from this model in mainstream asset management are as follows.

Index Tracking Funds

These funds have grown in popularity in recent years due to the difficulties some fund managers have had in outperforming market indices, and a growing awareness by investors generally that the long term trend for equity markets is upwards. Some asset management houses have, therefore, introduced products which simply aim to provide the investor with exposure to the overall market, without the 'added value' of selecting stocks within each market that the fund manager thinks will perform better than others. One attraction for investors is the lower management fee generally charged for this type of fund (because of the lower amount of work required from the fund manager).

The index tracking fund will aim to mirror the index on which it is based as closely as possible by investing in the index's constituent securities. The ideal would be to invest in every single security, in proportions reflecting the relative market capitalizations of the companies included in, for example, the FTSE 100 index. Thus the fund manager would simply need periodically to rebalance his portfolio to adjust the portfolio back in line with the index (eg monthly when new index figures are published).

However, it is not always possible for the fund manager to invest in each and every security. If, for example, he was looking to track the FT All Share index he may not have a sufficiently large fund to make it feasible for him to invest in all of the 700+ constituent securities. In this instance he will have to structure his portfolio to track the index as closely as he can. This might involve selecting securities with a beta around one, trying to maintain an overall portfolio weighted beta of as close to one as possible, monitoring the tracking error of the fund versus the index and taking appropriate action.

Hedge Funds

Hedge funds differ from normal funds only in that the fund manager is permitted to take short positions in stocks that he thinks will fall in value, in addition to taking 'normal' long positions.

The main administrative issue is that there is a requirement to borrow stock in order to deliver it against the short position taken.

Administration

There is a significant amount of administrative work that must be carried out by the fund manager and his assistants to ensure the smooth running and full investment of the fund.

Current holdings within the fund will, from time to time, generate dividend payments, which need to be reinvested. This is important since fund managers are generally measured against total return indices, which assume that dividends are reinvested in the market. In addition, valuable rights issues and other corporate actions may occur, which require the fund manager's attention. Initial Public Offerings (IPOs) may also be offered to the fund manager, which need to be properly administered to meet with various compliance rules.

When carrying out orders on behalf of the client, the fund managers must ensure that all regulatory checks are carried out on a pre-trade basis (eg whether a trade would take a unitized vehicle over 5% invested in one particular company). Also checked on a pre-trade basis are any client specific restrictions, such as those preventing the fund manager from investing in firms involved in 'unethical' businesses such as tobacco production or weapons manufacture. In addition, the fund manager must ensure that all client dealing is carried out before any deals are transacted on behalf of himself, or his firm, and that all clients are treated equally (eg they all receive the same price for securities traded in the market). From a post-trade perspective, the fund manager must comply with the requirements for corporate ownership reporting as specified in the Companies Act, and as laid down in Stock Exchange Rule 8 relating to holdings over a given percentage of the issued capital of a firm. Asset management firms may actually introduce this as a pre-trade check (ie making sure that their holdings do not breach these thresholds), thereby avoiding the need to publicly declare their large positions to the market.

Most funds apart from pension funds are subject to taxation. A fund manager must keep the implications of his client's tax position in mind when making investment decisions, and also at year end. In general, the fund manager should try to avoid selling positions which would result in a large capital gain (as calculated by the sale value less the purchase value). One way to mitigate this liability is to 'bed and breakfast' a stock building up a large capital gain by selling it on the last day of the tax year and buying it back on the first day of the next. In this way the capital gain is spread over a number of tax years.

CHAPTER 8

Fixed Interest Fund Management

Introduction

'Fixed interest', 'fixed income' or 'bond' funds provide a useful alternative to other forms of investment, particularly equities, with which fixed interest markets have traditionally had a fairly low correlation of volatility of returns[23], thereby offering portfolio diversification opportunities. The investor gets a significant proportion of the return in the form of a guaranteed, fixed income stream in terms of coupons. This contrasts with equity markets where there is an increasing trend towards lower dividend yields. A bond fund holder can also enjoy an element of capital return through price increases and switching between bonds.

Bonds tend to represent a lower risk option, in terms of price volatility, which is particularly important for some investors. In particular, older members of pension funds will want to protect their final pension fund value as far as possible, and will tend to switch from equities to bonds as they approach retirement. Bond portfolios are also attractive for investors requiring a stable income stream (rather than high capital growth potential).

Similarly to equities, the premise of fixed interest fund management is that the combination of a group, or portfolio, of bonds offers a superior risk-adjusted investment opportunity to individual bonds. This diversification is achieved through investing across different categories, such as markets (as defined by the currency in which the bond is denominated), industrial sectors (for corporate bonds) and the yield curve (using maturity buckets).

---

[23] Bond and equity market returns were found to have a correlation coefficient of 0.21 (ie a low positive correlation) between 1926 and 1991 by Statman and Ushman (JPM 1987).

These categories represent some of the different sources of risk and return to bond portfolios, at which we will be taking a detailed look later in this chapter.

Fixed interest analysts tend to make more use of 'technical analysis' type tools, such as charts showing trends of moving averages of yields, yield spreads etc, than their equity counterparts. These models have been found to provide useful forecasts of future market behaviour.

Like all markets, current expectations are already factored in (or 'priced into the curve' in fixed interest jargon). Actual events, such as interest rate changes, may have the opposite effect to that expected. For example, an interest rate cut may actually cause bond prices to fall, due to the fact that the cut was smaller than that expected, because the cut may be viewed as being better news for equities – leading to a net capital flow out of equities into bonds, or due to inflation fears (which would particularly affect the long end of the market).

Key Characteristics of Bonds

Before starting the following section it is important to be clear about the relationship between bond prices and bond yields. In the fixed interest market, the main metric for how the market is doing is yield. This is because it is easy to compare the yields of two bonds to decide which is 'cheaper' (simply by looking for the higher yield). In addition, yields can be compared to other market interest rates (eg LIBOR). It is changes to these market rates that will result in changes to prices of bonds. Thus if market rates rise, the yields on all bonds will be less attractive than they were previously and the prices of all bonds will fall.

If we first consider an individual bond, the key basic features for an investor are as follows.

Vanilla Bonds
Yield
Bonds provide a stream of cash flows to the bond holder over the life of the bond. These cash flows are used to calculate an interest rate to the bond's maturity date, which is generally referred to as its 'yield' in bond

markets. Most bonds are 'plain vanilla', ie they have no special embedded options or changing collateral base. In this case the yield is very simple to calculate, being simply the coupon rate divided by the price.

Using a very simple example of a five year bond currently priced at £90 with a coupon rate of £9.00 per annum which we purchase now (ie end of year 0) for £110:

End of Year	0	1	2	3	4	5
Cash Flow	−110	9	9	9	9	109

The yield to maturity is actually quite complex to calculate. It is the rate of interest such that when this rate is used to discount the positive cash flows from year 1 onwards, it gives a net present value of these cash flows equal to the price (this is really the internal rate of return of the bond). For our 9% coupon bond the yield is calculated by solving the following equation for y:

$$\text{Price} = 110 = \frac{9}{1+y} + \frac{9}{(1+y)^2} + \frac{9}{(1+y)^3} + \frac{9}{(1+y)^4} + \frac{109}{(1+y)^5}$$

Which here is 6.59%, being the rate of return we will be earning on a per annum basis through investing in this security. This rate of interest can be used to compare investing in this bond to other forms of investment, and deciding whether the difference in return is acceptable given the relative risk profiles of each investment opportunity. Thus if this bond was issued by a corporation with a poor default history, we might prefer to invest in a government bond offering a lower yield of 3.8% but which offered less risk of us not receiving our cash flows and principal. Yields can also be used for a more general purpose to compare bond returns with equities and cash. Again it is the risk versus return trade-off that is important.

Bonds with special features

Where bonds have special features, adjustments to yield calculations are required. For example, where a call option exists, entitling the issuer to redeem the bond at or above par on a given date, bond analysts will usually calculate the yield to the worst case scenario (or 'yield to worst') for the bond. This yield measure will depend on the current price of the bond and interest rates prevalent at the time.

Thus, if there was an option available to the issuer to call our 9% coupon bond at par after three years, then, if market interest rates have fallen, the bond would probably be called, resulting in the following cash flows:

End of Year	0	1	2	3
Cash Flow	−110	9	9	109

The bond would be called because the issuer can refinance his debt at a lower rate of interest if he exercises this option. Obviously the investor is on the other side of this, and will experience a lower holding period return (of 5.31%[24]). In reality, of course, the impact of the existence of this option will be factored into the purchase price of the bond.

Similar calculations are made on bonds having features such as 'sinking funds'. These are securities whose underlying debt is repaid in tranches throughout the life of the bond. Examples of these include mortgage-backed debt (generally referred to as Collateralized Mortgage Obligations or CMOs) such as 'Ginnie Mae's' and 'Freddie Mac's'. 'Brady Bonds' issued by third world countries which allow for the early repayment of capital throughout the life of the bond are another example of sinking fund bonds.

Thus if our bond was structured in this way, it would have an explicit or estimated repayment schedule associated with it which would affect the yield of the bond, for example:

End of Year	0	1	2	3	4	5
Cash Flow on Outstanding Debt	−110	9	9	9	6	36.33
Repayment				33.33	33.33	
Overall Cash Flow	−110	9	9	42.33	39.33	36.33

The sinking fund feature reduces the yield on the bond to 6.09%, owing to the reducing coupon payments being made as the debt is gradually repaid.

---

[24] This is, of course, the worst case from the lender's (ie the fund manager's) perspective, since he will be forced to reinvest at a lower interest rate.

Price

As mentioned above, the price of bonds is entirely dependent on prevailing and expected changes to market interest rates and bond yields. The current market price is essentially the net present value of the bond's cash flows discounted using a series of market interest rates corresponding to the time between now and the receipt of each cash flow. The behaviour of prices given different market expectations with regard to this series of spot rates (generally referred to as the 'yield curve' or the 'term structure of interest rates') is covered in detail below. The important point is that bond prices are really a summation of each of its cash flows discounted by the relevant interest rate. Prices will, therefore fluctuate as interest rate expectations change. These interest rates are essentially consensus rates, ie the view of the market as a whole. The price will be calculated differently by each market player (asset managers, brokers, dealers etc) according to their interest rate expectations. Each house will model the price by discounting the bond's cash flows using their expected interest rate model, and building in expectations regarding other factors such as changes in inflation (which reduce the real value of future cash flows).

Bond prices are quoted either 'clean' or 'dirty'. Clean prices do not include accrued interest, which is the amount of interest earned by the bond since the last coupon payment. Dirty, or gross, prices do include accrued interest and are what will be paid for a bond (since the new owner will be entitled to collect the forthcoming coupon payment in its entirety despite the fact that he has not held it for the entire period to which the coupon relates). By paying the accrued interest element, the new owner of the bond is compensating the old owner for the amount of interest earned, but not received.

The dirty price actually provides a good deal of useful information about a bond. It enables analysts to calculate the performance of the bond, since a time-series of dirty prices reflects both the capital appreciation and interest aspects of a bond's returns, making it directly comparable with equity prices (which have expected dividend payments factored in). It also provides the basis for the calculation of the weighted exposures that each security represents in a portfolio.

The fact that bonds are always redeemed at par is another factor for consideration. The implication of this is that, whatever price a bond may rise or fall to during its life, it will be redeemed at par (generally 100 of the unit of denomination) at maturity. This feature is known as 'convergence' and becomes a very significant factor as a bond approaches maturity. Thus whether a bond is currently trading at a premium or discount to par, it will converge to par at maturity:

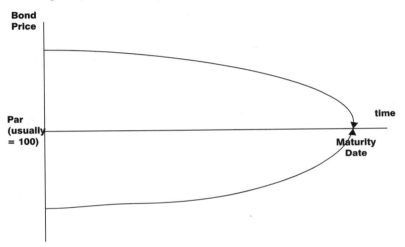

Time to Maturity

The length of time between now and the maturity date of the bond is another important measure. It is important because any change in important factors, such as interest rates, will have a much greater effect on the value of a bond's cash flows if the time between now and the receipt of a cash flow is longer.

This can be simply demonstrated by considering two very simple bonds, both of which are zero coupon, ie they pay a single cash flow at the end of their lives (ie at maturity). One matures in two years' time, the other in ten years. If interest rates start at 5% and rise to 6%, their respective prices will be as follows.

	Price 5%	Price 6%	Change (%)
Bond 2 Years	90.70	89.00	−1.88
Bond 10 Years	61.39	55.84	−9.04

Thus the 10 year bond's price has declined nearly *five times* more than the two year bond, given the same change in interest rates. This is simply explained by the fact that the discount factor used to calculate the net present value of the cash flow at maturity has increased by much more than that used to discount the two year bond.

Few bonds are as simple as this, however. Most pay coupons between purchase and maturity, all of which will be influenced by interest rates in the same way that the redemption payment was affected by a change in interest rates in the simple example given above. In order to provide a single measure of the time between now and the receipt of cash flows due to bond holders a weighted average time to maturity was proposed by Professor Frederick W. Macaulay in 1932.

This is simply calculated by weighting each of the discounted cash flows by its time (in years) to receipt. If we consider our two bonds again, but this time change their structure so that they pay a 10% coupon annually, then if interest rates are 5%, the weighted average time to maturity for each bond is calculated as follows.

Two Year Bond:

Year	1	2	Total
Cash Flow	10	110	
NPV	9.5	99.8	109.3
Weighted Time to Maturity	9.5	199.5	209.1

Ten Year Bond:

Year	1	2	3	4	5	6	7	8	9	10	Total
Cash Flow	10	10	10	10	10	10	10	10	10	110	
NPV	9.5	9.1	8.6	8.2	7.8	7.5	7.1	6.8	6.4	67.5	138.6
Weighted Time to Maturity	9.5	18.1	25.9	32.9	39.2	44.8	49.7	54.1	58.0	675.3	1007.7

Macaulay's measure of the weighted time to maturity, which he termed 'duration', is found by:

$$\frac{\Sigma(\text{Time} \times \text{CashFlowNPV})}{\Sigma \text{CashFlowNPV}}$$

Thus for the two year bond the duration is:

$$\frac{209.1}{109.3} = 1.91$$

and for the 10 year bond it is:

$$\frac{1007.7}{138.6} = 7.27$$

Although not perfect by any means, Macaulay's duration enables bond analysts to compare the risk of different bonds in the market (eg of adverse interest rate changes, or inflation increases).

We will be looking at the uses of duration in greater depth later in this chapter; the most important point for now is that fund managers need to have an idea of what impact a change in interest rates is likely to have on their portfolios. Analogously to an equity's beta, the higher the duration, the greater the level of market risk.

The Term Structure of Interest Rates

As mentioned above, the term structure of interest rates, or yield curve, is the key to the market price of bonds. It plots a series of rates of interest for agreeing to lend/borrow from now until a series of dates in the future. It is expectations of changes to this term structure that drive movements in bond prices. These expectations are those of market analysts assimilating economic and other data, and interpreting this data to forecast market changes.

In the diagram below, a series of interest rates for agreeing to lend from now to a series of time periods is plotted. Thus, the rate for lending from now for three years is 6.80% p.a., whereas the rate for lending for ten years is 7.55%

'Normal' Yield Curve Shape

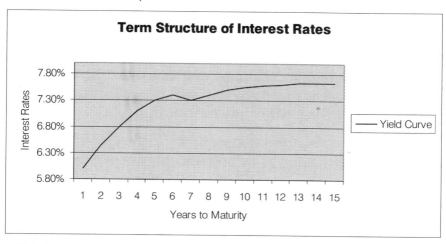

This is termed 'normal' since it is usually expected that a higher yield is available for longer lending due to inflation uncertainty. The frequently observed kink at around seven years' maturity is held to exist due to supply and demand conditions in the market eg the interaction between banks (who prefer to lend short) and insurance companies (who prefer to borrow long). The kink represents the upper limit for short lenders and the lower limit for long borrowers who will lend/borrow only if rates are very favourable. The result of this tends to be a short supply, leading to a lower yield.

Expected changes to this term structure will have the following impact.

Yield Curve Change	Bond Price Impact	Notes
General shift upwards	Falls	Investor will shorten duration of portfolios in order that he can reinvest as soon as possible at the higher rate
General shift downwards	Rises	Investor will lengthen duration of portfolios in order that higher yield enjoyed for longer
Steepening	Generally will fall	Depends on bond maturity and 'pivot point' of steepening curve
Flattening	Generally will rise	Depends on bond maturity and 'pivot point' of flattening curve

Bond Price Behaviour

An important point to note is that if a bond is held to maturity, then the changes in the price of the bond are of no consequence. The investor still receives the coupon payments and the par amount at maturity, and therefore realizes the yield promised by the bond at the time of purchase. Whether this yield represents a competitive return compared to other available investments is another matter, however.

Fixed interest fund management generally involves a great deal of transaction activity (ie buying and selling bonds in the market). This is because views on interest rates are changing, resulting in the frequent restructuring of portfolios. Additionally the fund manager will be looking for 'switching' opportunities (selling a bond looking 'expensive' or 'rich' and buying a bond looking 'cheap') according to the house interest rate view. Another incentive for active management is that transaction costs are relatively low compared to equities.

Let us start by analysing the effect of interest rate change on an individual bond, say a bond currently priced at 100, with annual coupon payments of 10 and with 10 years to maturity. If it was a UK Government Issue, it might be called 'Treasury 10% 2012'. The cash flows from this bond would be as follows.

End of Year	1	2	3	4	5	6	7	8	9	10
Cash Flow	10	10	10	10	10	10	10	10	10	110

The final cash flow consists of the final coupon payment and the repayment of the principal.

The value (or price) of this bond will be calculated by market players by using their own expectations of future interest rates (ie their projected yield curve, illustrated in the diagram below). They will calculate this by discounting each cash flow using the appropriate expected interest rate for the period in which the cash flow falls.

Starting with the simplest (and also least realistic) scenario where interest rates are 10% for every time period:

End of Year	1	2	3	4	5	6	7	8	9	10	Total
Cash Flow	10	10	10	10	10	10	10	10	10	110	
Interest Rate	10	10	10	10	10	10	10	10	10	10	
Discount Factor	0.91	0.83	0.75	0.68	0.62	0.56	0.51	0.47	0.42	0.39	
NPV of Cash Flows	9.09	8.26	7.51	6.83	6.21	5.64	5.13	4.67	4.24	42.41	100.00

As might be expected, given this flat yield curve at 10%, the price of the bond is 100.

Let us say that the yield curve 'steepens' into a more normal shape, as represented by the following table.

End of Year	1	2	3	4	5	6	7	8	9	10	Total
Cash Flow	10	10	10	10	10	10	10	10	10	110	
Interest Rate	7.5	8	8.5	9	9.5	10	10.5	11	11.5	12	
Discount Factor	0.93	0.86	0.78	0.71	0.64	0.56	0.50	0.43	0.38	0.32	
NPV of Cash Flows	9.30	8.57	7.83	7.08	6.35	5.64	4.97	4.34	3.75	35.42	93.27

As can be seen, the price of the bond has fallen. This is largely because the interest rate used to discount the largest cash flow (the final coupon plus redemption payment) has increased from 10% to 12%. The fall in the interest rates used to discount the earlier coupon payments does not compensate for this since the impact on the Discount Factors is less (since there are fewer compounding periods) and the cash flows are smaller. The key to the impact of the yield curve shape change on the price is the 'positioning' of each particular bond on the yield curve, this being approximated by the concept of duration, which we will address shortly.

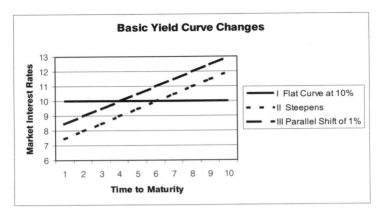

Let us now see what happens when interest rates rise by 1% (we'll assume, unrealistically, that interest rates for all maturities change by the same amount, ie a parallel yield curve shift).

End of Year	1	2	3	4	5	6	7	8	9	10	Total
Cash Flow	10	10	10	10	10	10	10	10	10	110	
Interest Rate	8.5	9	9.5	10	10.5	11	11.5	12	12.5	13	
Discount Factor	0.92	0.84	0.76	0.68	0.61	0.53	0.47	0.40	0.35	0.29	
NPV of Cash Flows	9.22	8.42	7.62	6.83	6.07	5.35	4.67	4.04	3.46	32.40	88.07

Here we can see that the price has fallen by just over 5.5%. The fall is to be expected since the NPV of all cash flows has fallen. However, the important metric is how much this bond has fallen compared to others.

To make this comparison, let us consider the impact of these interest rate changes on another bond, for example a bond that matures in five, rather than ten, years.

Cash Flow	10	10	10	10	110	
Interest Rate	7.5	8	8.5	9	9.5	
Discount Factor	0.93	0.86	0.78	0.71	0.64	
NPV of Cash Flows	9.30	8.57	7.83	7.08	70.40	103.2
Interest Rate	8.5	9	9.5	10	10.5	
Discount Factor	0.92	0.84	0.76	0.68	0.61	
NPV of Cash Flows	9.22	8.42	7.62	6.83	67.1	99.2

The fall in the price of the bond of 3.9% is markedly lower than the 5.5% fall in the longer dated bond. The reverse would be true if market interest rates fell across the board; in which case the price of the longer dated bond would rise more than that of the shorter dated bond. Thus the longer dated bond is more *sensitive*[25] to interest rate changes than the shorter dated bond. Another factor is that if interest rates rise, fund managers will wish to reinvest at this higher rate as soon as possible. The implication of this is that, if an interest rate rise is expected, fund managers will adjust their portfolios to enable them to reinvest earlier[26].

Key Fixed Interest Risk and Return Measures

Now that we have examined the influences upon the bond market in greater detail, let us revisit the important metrics in fixed interest fund management.

Measures of Return

Yield

The yield on a bond essentially answers the following question: 'if I buy a bond now and hold it until maturity, what return will I get?' This provides a useful comparative measure, when comparing bonds at the time of choosing between bonds to buy or sell into a portfolio, for a historic time series view of one bond, and for the bond market as a whole against equity markets. This measure of yield is variously known as 'yield to maturity' or 'redemption yield'. Where, however, there are options embedded in the bonds, it may be imprudent to assume that the bond will continue to pay coupons until its maturity date. Fund managers will, therefore, use a 'yield to worst', 'yield to next call' or similar prudent return measure when analysing a bond's attractiveness, ie generally on a worst case scenario basis.

Holding period return

Of course bonds are not always held from purchase until redemption, often being the subject of a 'switch' into a cheaper bond. The price of the bond generally fluctuates during its life as market forces impinge upon it.

---

[25] This sensitivity is measured by modified duration or volatility.

[26] Fund managers will look at the Macaulay's duration, which is the cash flow weighted average time to maturity of a bond (or portfolio of bonds), of their fund and reduce the duration if they think that rates will rise and increase it (eg by buying longer dated bonds) if they think rates will fall.

This means that the yield will be an inaccurate measure of the return actually received from the bond when viewed retrospectively. If we consider a new issue five year bond bought at a price of 100 when yields and interest rates (and the coupon rate) were 8% and then sold two years later when interest rates had risen to 10%, and the price of the bond had additionally fallen due to increased supply in its sector, the return might have been as follows.

Cash Flow/ Calculation
Return

Initial Outlay	−100	
Coupons Received	16	
Price Received upon Disposal	93.03	NPV of cash flows for years 3 to 5 = 95.03, further reduction of 2 due to supply factors
Holding Period Return	4.42%	

Thus yield is generally a forward-looking measure of promised return on a stock by stock basis, whereas the holding period return (here very disappointingly lower than that anticipated initially) is a retrospective view of the actual return by the fund manager achieved over a given period.

Measures of Risk

In recent years, bond analysts have moved from using Macaulay's Duration as their main measure of overall market risk in favour of modified duration, which is sometimes referred to as volatility. Although these measures are actually very closely related, they measure completely different concepts and provide information for quite different purposes in fixed interest fund management.

Similarly to yield measures, duration figures vary according to assumptions made regarding optionality and other special features embedded in some bonds. Thus bonds with sinking funds or call options will generally have their durations adjusted downwards to account for these features. The convention for floating rate instruments such as Floating Rate Notes (FRNs) (where the interest rate is not completely fixed, but 'floats' above a benchmark or reference rate such as LIBOR) is that the duration is assumed to be to the next reset date, this being the date at which the interest rate is fixed through reference to the benchmark rate.

Macaulay's Duration

Macaulay's Duration is the weighted average time to receipt of cash flows due to the bond holder, the largest of which is obviously at maturity. This gives the fund manager an indication of the bond (or fund's) position on the yield curve. In general, this provides fund managers with a useful metric for making decisions; eg if they expect interest rates to rise they will want to reduce the average time (ie move the portfolio back down the yield curve) until they receive their cash flows in order that they can reinvest at a higher interest rate. This measure is utilized much less in the management of bond funds that are simply looking to maximize their returns from the markets in which they invest. Thus a sterling bond OEIC will aim to achieve the greatest holding period return from all government and corporate bonds denominated in sterling. In this case the fund manager is mainly interested in the impact of interest rate changes on the prices of bonds, and therefore the overall value of the portfolio.

Many bond funds exist in order to provide the fund's owners with a stream of cash flows. Examples of this might be pension holders looking for a monthly income stream, life companies who have to pay out benefits to holders or their dependants or insurance companies who need to pay cash out of their fund to meet claims. These payments are termed 'liabilities', and are generally calculated by actuaries who will define a liability stream using past data on average pension entitlement take up (eg lump sum versus annuity ratios), death rates etc. The bond fund manager's job is to ensure that these liability streams are adequately covered by the cash flows generated by the fund (mainly from maturity of bonds and receipt of coupons), and that the value of the cash flows is protected from interest rate changes and inflation.

A very simple example might be the setting of the following liability stream calculated by the appointed actuaries from the probable requirements of the fund's beneficiaries.

RTP Pension Fund – Liabilities

Beneficiary	Date	Amount Payable
J B Evans, Esq	02/04/2002	3,143,000
A R Wagg, Esq	16/07/2007	2,230,000
G A Kerr, Esq	01/06/2024	5,678,000
A D B Hughes, Esq	20/04/2028	3,878,000

In this very simple example, the prospective pensioners have elected to take their entitlement in the form of a lump sum. The amount payable is obviously an estimate and will be subject to considerable potential fluctuation particularly for the younger participants who are probably still largely invested in equities. However, if these estimates were correct and the capital was available, the fund manager would have a relatively easy job; he would simply need to invest the fund's capital in a series of four bonds maturing in the required amounts on the retirement dates specified. Life is never this easy, however. The following factors make the fund manager's job complex:

> ▶ It is unlikely that the funds for the later retirees will be available yet. The funds will need to remain in the faster growing equity markets before they reach the required pension level. The fund manager cannot predict with any certainty what will happen in the future, and may face a shortfall

> ▶ Even for the closer dated payments, it is unlikely that bonds will be available with the exact retirement date

> ▶ For a number of reasons, the pension entitlement amount or the date on which it is taken may change (eg early retirement)

Thus the fund manager will probably have to have a balanced portfolio initially, moving more into bonds when the amounts and dates become more certain and/or when the capital value of the fund has reached the required level.

This gives the liability matching fund manager a very different focus to that of an OEIC manager. He is much less concerned with the sensitivity of the fund's value in the event that interest rates fall, and much more interested in the impact of the interest rate change on his cash flow stream. The main issue that the fund manager has to to contend with for this type of fund revolves around the maintenance of the cash flows at the required level in the event of a change in interest rates. The most common technique used is 'immunization'. This is achieved by setting the Macaulay's Duration of the portfolio to be the same as the Macaulay's Duration of the liability stream. The idea behind this is that, whatever the change in interest rates experienced, the fund will continue to be able provide the cash flows required to meet the liability stream calculated by the actuaries. In general, if interest rates rise then the capital value of the fund will fall, but the fund manager will be able to reinvest cash flows received at a higher rate of interest. If interest rates fall, the fund manager will enjoy a capital appreciation in the price of the fund, but will be reinvesting his cash flow receipts at a lower rate of interest.

This immunization technique is only fully effective for parallel yield curve shifts. If the yield curve changes shape, the fund manager can no longer guarantee to meet the requirements of the liability stream. In fact the only way that a fund manager can guarantee to meet the liability stream is to match it cash flow for cash flow, ensuring that there is no 'reinvestment risk' (ie that he will be forced to reinvest at a lower yield at some point in the future).

Modified Duration

Modified duration, or volatility, measures the expected change in the price of a bond for a *small*[27] change in interest rates. As mentioned above, this is the key measure used by managers of funds looking to maximize the holding period return of their fund. For these managers, a rise in interest rates will have a negative effect on the performance of the fund. The key is to beat the fund benchmark's performance. In general terms this can be achieved by being longer than the index (in weighted modified duration terms) when interest rates fall (and consequently bond markets rise), and shorter than the index at the point when interest rates rise.

Weighted duration gives a measure of the sensitivity of either an individual bond, or of a portfolio of bonds, to a change in interest rates. The key risk

[27] For large changes in interest rates, the 'convexity' of the bond needs to be taken into account. This concept is covered in Appendix IV.

measure for bond fund managers is how they are positioned against their benchmark; thus they will be looking to see what their relative position is against the benchmark. This type of analysis is generally carried out in more detail through breaking the portfolio down by grouping bonds with similar characteristics. Common categories used for grouping are currency of denomination[28], issuer type (eg government, investment grade, or high yield[29]), credit ratings and maturity.

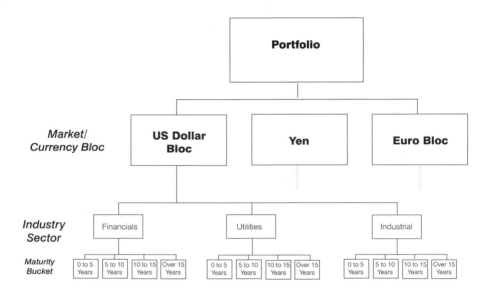

Analysts will use covariance matrix analysis to identify diversification opportunities between buckets (eg bonds with between 0 to 5 years' maturity may have a low correlation of volatility of returns with 10–15 year bonds in a given market).

Other Fixed Interest Management Issues

In addition to the strategic issues concerning fixed interest fund

[28] It is important to note that the currency of denomination is exactly that, and nothing to do with the issuer. Thus a 'Kingdom of Sweden 5.25% 2012' bond issued by the Swedish government in US dollars forms part of the US dollar bond market, rather than the European bond market. The reason for this is that the behaviour of this bond will mainly be influenced by US domestic interest rates, rather than Swedish interest rates.

[29] High yield bonds are also referred to as speculative grade, or more colloquially as 'junk'. Fund managers will compare the amount of weighted duration, ie the market risk that they have in each category, with the weighted duration of the benchmark.

management, there are a number of other risk factors and issues that have to be managed. On a day to day basis, the fund manager will have to look at the overall duration of his fund against the benchmark and adjust his position on the basis of his/the house view on interest rates. In addition he will have to look at the distribution of his fund across the market in terms of currency, maturity bucket and industry allocations.

At the same time, there are other analytical and administrative tasks which must be carried out in order that the fund manager controls his risk effectively, and ensures that the fund runs smoothly.

Flight to Quality as Nominal Interest Rates Rise

As yields rise, the cost of borrowing obviously increases, but beyond a certain level it puts great deal of pressure on higher risk borrowers such as low credit rated corporates and third world governments. The key factor in a rising interest rate scenario is that borrowers become less and less able to meet coupon payments. This increases the likelihood of default either on coupon payments, redemption amounts or both. The ensuing 'flight to quality' as lenders seek to avoid the increasing risk of default results in a further hike in yields (resulting from the fall in prices caused by the lower demand). This phenomenon has serious implications for portfolio managers invested in high yield bonds since they will be facing both falling prices and an increasing risk of default.

'Barbelling[30]'

Often fund managers will want to invest in longer dated bonds that they perceive as being cheap. The problem is that he needs to balance off the increase in duration that the purchase of this longer dated instrument would otherwise cause. In order to do this he will simultaneously buy an amount of a short-dated instrument (eg one with three months remaining to maturity), in order that the net effect on the fund's overall duration is that required by the fund manager. Let's consider a scenario where a £100,000,000 fund manager wants to add a weighted duration of 0.9 years to his fund, has £10,000,000 to invest and feels that the Treasury 9% 2028, which has a duration of 17.75 years, is looking cheap at 101.25. If the fund manager simply invests the £10,000,000 in the bond, he will add the following duration to the fund:

[30] 'Barbelling'simply means that securities which are some distance from each other on the yield curve are viewed as being part of the same strategy, being fancifully compared to a weightlifter's barbell, eg: see diagram on page 112.

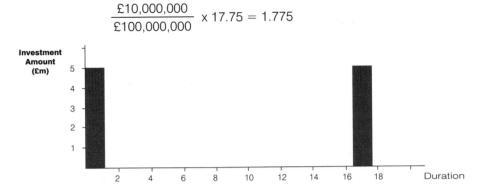

$$\frac{£10,000,000}{£100,000,000} \times 17.75 = 1.775$$

This is obviously a long way from the 0.9 years target. However, by 'barbelling' this security with another with negligible duration, such as a three month Bill, we can achieve the required weighted duration from the £10,000,000 investment as follows.

Instrument	Investment Amount	Fund Weight	Duration	Weighted Duration
3 Month T-Bill	5,000,000	5%	0.25	0.0125
Treasury 9% 2028	5,000,000	5%	17.75	0.8875
Total	10,000,000	10%		0.9

The key here is to ensure that the money market or cash instrument used for the barbell remains in the portfolio. If it matures and the cash is spent, there is a risk that the portfolio will exceed its intended risk profile in terms of weighted duration.

Corporate Bonds

Credit Rating Changes

Credit rating services are provided by such companies as Standard and Poor's and Moody's and express a relative measure of a company's likelihood of defaulting on its repayment obligations with respect to debt instruments issued by that company. The ratings range from AAA, where a corporation has a very low chance of defaulting, through to C or D ratings where issuers are considered to have a high chance of defaulting. Whereas analysts assess whether the higher yield offered by C or D rated (or 'junk') bonds justifies the risk of default (ie not actually receiving the coupons or principal paid out), they will be more concerned with the risk of downgrading of higher rated bonds. A downgrade of an AAA rated bond (which should be a fairly safe bet since one of the requirements of this rating is that a large amount of cash needs to be held by the company) to an AA rating will result in a fall in the price of the bond and a capital loss to the investor. It is this risk (seen in the recent past with BT debt issues) that the analyst will assess for each corporate bond.

Similarly to equity fund managers, corporate bondholders need to monitor news items affecting the companies whose debt they are holding. They are interested in any news item that might affect the credit rating of a corporation, eg worse than expected results, cash flow problems, resignation of key executives etc. In addition to a full change of credit rating, companies are often put on 'creditwatch' where ratings agencies such as Moody's and Standard and Poor's may have received some unconfirmed information about the company. This may precede a full change to the company's rating. The revision of credit ratings (these are usually colloquially expressed in terns of 'notches', where a change from A+ to A would be one notch, and A+ to A- would be two notches) will obviously have a huge effect on the price of the bond.

Corporate Yield Analysis

Bond analysts break yields on corporate bonds down into three elements.

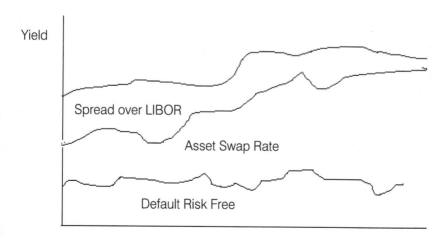

The default risk free yield is that offered by a government security with similar characteristics (eg roughly the same time to maturity, profile etc). The asset swap rate is the rate offered in exchange for moving away from the safety of government debt, this rate being calculated on the basis of AA rated paper. The spread over LIBOR or 'margin' is a company specific measure, representing the borrowing rate for this particular corporate over the benchmark overnight rate. Analysts will monitor the relationships between these rates using time series data, with a view to identifying patterns in the data. In particular, they are looking to see whether the spread or margin is narrowing, being an indicator that the trend of the bond's price will be upward.

'Coupon Washing'

Many funds have to pay tax on income earned; in the case of bonds income is received in the form of coupon payments. In agreement with his client, the fund manager may avoid payment of tax on this income by selling the bond just before it 'goes XD', ie it becomes entitled to a dividend. He will then buy it back again just after the XD date. The (dirty) price that he sells it for will include accrued interest that has been earned on the bond, so the net effect is really that he is capitalizing income earned.

Reinvestment

The reinvestment of income, where received from either coupons or redemption payments, represents a risk to the portfolio, since it may not be possible for the fund manager to reinvest these cash receipts at the same rate of interest currently being earned on the bond (eg if yields have generally fallen). For this reason zero coupon bonds can be attractive, since they cut down the number of times that the fund manager has to reinvest cash flows received.

CHAPTER 9

Currency Management

Introduction

Currency management focuses on seeking to obtain returns by managing the risk of changes to foreign exchange (FX) rates. Foreign exchange risk occurs whenever a fund manager is holding assets denominated in a currency other than the fund's base currency. These asset's returns can be viewed as being derived from two sources: firstly from changes to the price of the asset in local currency terms and secondly, from changes to the level of the currency. If managers are concerned about the immediate prospects for the currency, they may well hedge their foreign exchange exposure, while leaving the underlying asset holding in place.

The management of currency risk differs from other asset management activities in the following ways. Firstly currency exposure is derived from holdings in other assets (equities, bonds, property cash etc). For currency management purposes, exposures from all of these asset classes are grouped together by currency as in the table opposite.

The fund manager will compare this summarized position with the current house view on prospects for each currency and, in some instances, with a specific currency exposure benchmark. If he wishes to change his position, he will move the fund into line with his desired currency position through purchasing or selling forward foreign exchange contracts. These are commitments to buy or sell a pair of currencies (eg 'buy US dollar, sell sterling') at a pre-agreed exchange rate at an agreed time in the future. The effect of these contracts is that, for the period of time that the contracts are in place, the fund manager will have increased his exposure to one currency and reduced his exposure to the other.

Underlying Asset Class	Asset Weight	Currency Weight	Currency
UK Equities	55.3	75.0	Sterling
Property	1.7		
UK Bonds	11.5		
Cash Sterling	6.5		
US Equities	5.7	8.0	US Dollar
US Bonds	2.3		
Japan Equities	6.4	6.4	Yen
Europe ex-UK Equities	10.6	10.6	Euro
Total	*100.0*	*100.0*	*Total*

Currency management is often referred to as an 'overlay' management process, ie 'overlaying' underlying security positions with forward FX contracts to achieve a desired net currency exposure. A significant factor is the relative ease with which fund managers can change their currency positions. FX markets are highly liquid, particularly for major currencies, making it very easy to make huge changes to exposures. There is an interesting trade-off when looking at fixed interest funds. If interest rates rise in, for example, Japan, the normal effect will be that bonds fall in value, but at the same time the yen will appreciate. Thus for a sterling-based fund the interesting metric is the *net* effect of these two influences on the value of the fund.

FX rates are quoted as either 'spot' (generally settling in two days from the trade being struck) or 'forward' (generally settling any time up to one year from trade date). It is the current spot rate that is used to calculate the current value of holdings denominated in currencies other than the fund base currency, whilst forward rates are those for agreeing *now* to exchange an amount of one currency for another at a point in the future, essentially locking the fund into the current market exchange rate.

FX rates usually move in the same direction as the currency's relevant domestic interest rate (ie US domestic interest rates for US dollars, Japanese rates for yen etc). The close relationship between foreign exchange levels and relative interest rates (ie the difference between domestic interest rates pertaining to different currencies) is explained by the covered interest arbitrage theory. This theory also enables one to calculate forward foreign exchange rates from spot exchange rates and interest rate differentials. Covered interest arbitrage is outlined in Appendix II.

FX rates are generally quoted in terms of the US dollar, which acts as the global financial world's reference currency. 'Cross rates' are also quoted between most major currencies, eg sterling/yen, euro/yen etc. The market is dominated by the major currencies, which are the US dollar, yen and euro. The main new development in recent years is the hugely ambitious euro project. An overview of the implications of this project is contained in Appendix V.

The performance of an FX trade is calculated as a profit or loss figure. The two sides of the trade are converted back into the base currency of the fund, for both from their initial cost and their current value. The total of these conversions gives the profit and loss on the trade. Thus, the manager of a sterling-based fund might want to hedge £20,000,000 of his US dollar exposure for a period of 6 months since he feels that the US dollar may fall sharply, creating a heavy loss from the US equity and fixed interest positions held in the fund. For simplicity's sake, let us say that interest rates in the UK and US are both 5% respectively, and that the current spot rate is 1.6250. The forward rate for six months in this scenario will, therefore, also be 1.6250 (there being no interest rate differential). Let us say that the fund manager has got it right, and the dollar does fall in value (against sterling), so that the spot rate is 1.6350 at the end of the six months. The profit from the trade will be calculated as follows.

Value	US$ Fund Segment (In Sterling)	Hedge Position (Sold US Dollar)	Conversion Rate	Hedge Position (Bought Sterling)
At Start of Contract	20,000,000	−32,500,000	1.6250	+20,000,000
At End of Contract	19,877,676	−32,500,000	1.6350	+19,877,676
Profit/Loss	−122,324			+122,324

Thus the fund manager is compensated for the lower value of his underlying holdings due to the depreciation of the US dollar relative to the base currency of the fund by a profit on his forward FX deal. Of course, there's no such thing as a free lunch: if the currency had appreciated the fund manager would have made a loss on the FX deal, thereby missing out on a potentially valuable contribution to the overall performance of his funds. In addition there would be a (relatively small) transaction cost for the hedge.

Currency Analysis

For the purposes of making allocations and controlling risk, currencies are generally grouped into 'blocs', these being groups of currencies with high correlations of volatility of returns. An example hierarchy might be as in the diagram opposite.

This hierarchy would be established by currency analysts, who would identify patterns of co-movements amongst currencies. The portfolio manager would seek to diversify his currency risk across these currency blocs as far as possible, for the same reasons that he will seek to diversify the holdings underlying the currency risks, that is to achieve superior risk adjusted returns.

Dealing and Administration

As mentioned above, currency management is carried out by means of forward FX trades. These are generally carried out in pairs of currencies (eg buy sterling forward, sell Japanese yen forward) simultaneously bought and sold forward to the same date for a pre-agreed amount. It is obviously important that these positions are 'rolled over' upon maturity, ie the currency overlay positions are maintained (if required) by the fund manager. Depending upon whether the fund manager has made a profit or loss on the FX trade, he may need to 'top up' the FX positions at this rollover point out of cash.

The forward FX contract obliges the fund manager to deliver a pre-set amount of the sold currency (US$ 32,500,000 in our earlier example) and to receive in exchange a pre-set amount of the bought currency (£20,000,000). In order to do this, the fund manager will need to ensure

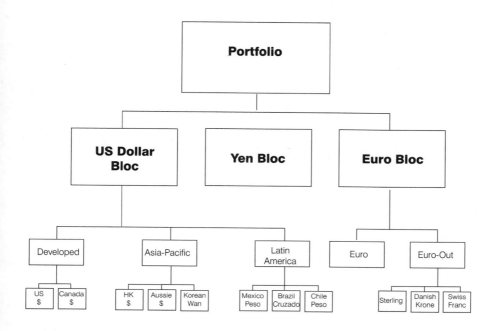

that he will be able to transfer the sold currency on the maturity date. He needs to generate two spot FX deals (which will be at the prevailing spot rate six months after the forward deal was struck in our example) in order to ensure that settlement can take place.

The series of trades/actions will, therefore, be as follows.

	Action	Buy/Receive	Sell/Deliver
Day 1	Six Month Forward FX Trade	£20,000,000	$32,500,000
Day 180	Spot Trade	$32,500,000	£19,877,676
Day 182	Cash Settlement	£20,000,000	$32,500,000

CHAPTER 10

Dealing, Cash Management and the Back Office

Introduction

These functions are generally seen as having a much lower status than the 'front office' investment management function. However, given that investment management companies are dealing with clients' money, it is of paramount importance that these functions are performed effectively. It is the failure to perform these functions adequately that is more likely to lead to an asset management company being heavily fined or closed down by the regulators than any malpractice in the front office.

Once fund managers have decided what they wish to buy or sell, they will instruct the asset management company dealers to execute a trade in the market with an external counterparty. These counterparties would be stockbrokers in the case of equities and bonds, a LIFFE member for futures or options, or an investment bank in the case of money market instruments, foreign exchange transactions, or interest rate swaps. Prior to issuing his instruction to his dealers, the fund manager would first check with the back office to ensure that the stock is available (if selling), or that cash is available (if buying). The back office would check its own records, and if necessary liaise with the custodian.

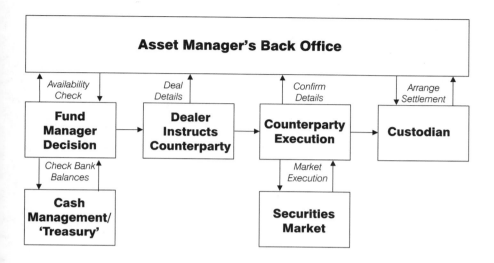

Once the dealer has agreed the transaction with his opposite number at the counterparty, the trade is passed on to the back office for confirmation and settlement. An additional task is liaison with the fund's custodian, who is responsible for the management of the 'physical' assets, primarily being stock certificates and bank account management. There is also a requirement for a 'global custodian' function, to cope with markets that do not allow stock certificates to leave the country (eg Japan). These certificates are held by the custodian in a 'depot' on the client's behalf in the securities' country of domicile. In any event it is generally more convenient for the securities to be held locally, since it expedites the settlement process.

Dealers

In addition to managing the deal execution process, the dealing team are also the asset management company's 'ear to the ground of the market' in terms of receiving information (such as the availability of parcels of cheap stock).

The functions of the dealing desk include the following.

Function	Notes
Trade execution 'at best'	Best available market price for that stock
Warehousing	Where not all of the required order can be met immediately, the dealer will arrange for the broker to 'warehouse' stock purchased so far. It is the responsibility of the dealer to ensure that all clients participating in the order receive the same price (being a weighted average of the prices obtained for each 'parcel')
Protection	The dealer can negotiate 'protection' from an adverse price change from its current price with the broker, if the asset management company is not quite ready to deal
Programme Trades	These are a series of trades grouped together and offered to a broker on the basis of better terms and conditions being negotiated by the dealer for this quantity of business

Dealers are not concerned with the client details, purely the 'bulk' side, ie how many to buy and sell in the market.

Cash Management

The objective of cash managers (also known as the 'Treasury Desk') is to achieve the maximum return for capital formally allocated by a fund manager to the cash security class. They are also responsible for the management of cash which is required for settlement in a number of days, but is available for investment now. Their role is to 'sweep' cash into Treasury Bills, Call Deposits, Short Term Income Funds (STIFs) or other money market instruments offering attractive interest rates. Since they are responsible for ensuring that the fund does not go overdrawn, they will often use a 'cash ladder' analysis to ensure that settlements are met without taking the fund into the red, or leaving cash uninvested overnight. The better the information the cash manager has at his disposal, the better the return that will be achieved (since higher rates are offered for funds committed for longer).

The idea behind a cash ladder is to give a temporal perspective on all cash expected to be received and required to be paid out, in order that the cash manager can ensure settlement whilst maximizing the fund's potential cash return. Thus, if for the sake of example today was Friday, 20 April, and we wanted to analyse the following series of events:

▶ Purchased £500,000 worth of UK equities yesterday

▶ Sell £250,000 worth of UK bonds

▶ Maturity of $600,000 worth of US dollar bonds on 27 April

▶ Notified of fund cash outflow of £300,000 for 23 April

If the fund's current 'cleared' cash position is £550,000, and we assume that settlement for UK equities is five days and for UK bonds two days and that the cable[31] rate is 1.6, a cash ladder analysis might look like this.

	Activity	Projected Cash
20 April		550,000
21 April		550,000
22 April		550,000
23 April	−300,000	250,000
24 April	250,000	500,000
25 April	−500,000	0
26 April		0
27 April	375,000	375,000

Given these events, the fund will not go overdrawn (although in practice, the cash manager would not be happy to be 'sailing as close to the wind' as this). In addition this tells the cash manager that he can put £300,000 on four days' call today (since it is not required until 25 April) and £250,000 on overnight deposit (weekends 'don't count'). In addition, the cash manager can provide guidance for the fund manager. Thus if the fund manager phones up and says that he wants to buy £350,000 worth of Hong Kong equity (which has a very short

[31] Cable is the dollar/sterling exchange rate.

settlement cycle of two days), the cash manager can use the cash ladder to carry out a 'what-if' to show the effect of this proposed action.

	Activity	*Projected Cash*
20 April		550,000
21 April		550,000
22 April		550,000
23 April	−650,000	−100,000
24 April	250,000	150,000
25 April	−500,000	−350,000
26 April		−350,000
27 April	375,000	25,000

Although the fund will end up in the black, it will go seriously overdrawn, which is usually unacceptable. The cash manager can advise the fund manager that, if he wants to go ahead now, he needs to simultaneously sell a security with a similar settlement period (eg UK bonds), otherwise he will have to wait until 25 April to trade.

Stock Lending

The Stock Lending department can earn useful revenue for client funds by temporarily loaning security certificates to market participants who wish to 'short' a stock ie sell a security that they do not currently own. Although the transaction is called a 'loan', it does involve the transfer of title (otherwise the borrowing investor would not be able to use it to settle in the market). However, unless otherwise agreed, the lender retains the benefits of the security (such as dividends, coupons etc). Stock Lending departments also get involved with borrowing stock where required, for example for hedge funds or where settlement problems have arisen.

Back Office

The 'back office' is a general name given to the department performing some of the less glamorous, but nonetheless vitally important, functions of an asset management house. Back office functions include the following:

Settlements

A slightly more accurate name might be 'settlement management', since the actual settlement of, for example, equity trades is carried out between the stockbroker who executed the trade in the market, and the custodian who looks after the client's physical assets (eg stock certificates) and cash. However, the asset manager's settlements department does confirm the trade against the broker's 'allegation' (ie what the broker thinks the trade is), and liaises with the global custodian with regard to any settlement issues (eg client's preferred settlement currency etc). The role of the settlements department is to ensure that all trades settle properly (eg that the security that the fund manager intended to buy ends up under the client's name at the custodian's vault), handling any mismatches by liaising directly with the broker. Custodial arrangements are sometimes complex, particularly for Private Clients having the same custodian (this is done to reduce the cost of custody for Private Clients). In this case trades carried out in the market are viewed very differently by the fund manager, dealers and settlements. Let us consider a series of transactions in Marks and Spencer carried out as a bulk order on behalf of the following Private Clients.

Client	Nominal	Custodian
Bedser	400	Chase
Botham	800	State Street
Laker	1,200	Barclays Global Investors
Larwood	600	Mellon
Snow	800	Chase
Trueman	250	Mellon
Willis	1,200	Barclays Global Investors

The transaction would be viewed in the following way by a fund manager, dealer and settlements department.

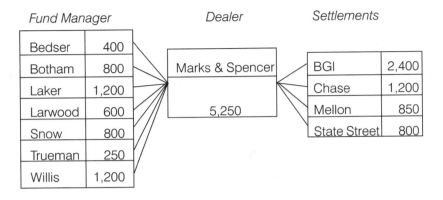

The role of the settlements department is to ensure that the correct number of certificates end up the correct custodial account or 'depot'.

Valuations

The correct and timely valuation of funds is extremely important, especially for unitized vehicles, for which market prices of units are based on valuations carried out by the asset management house's Valuations department. In addition, the valuation of portfolios for client reporting has increased in importance as the market becomes more competitive and as asset management houses seek to improve the quality of the service that they provide to their clients. In addition, the Valuations department provide information to internal users, particularly the fund managers and the Quants desk.

Valuations are carried out by calculating the value of each holding, including any accrued interest for bonds. The fund valuation is calculated from the sum of these individual security valuations, less any fees, charges, tax etc due to come out of the fund. One of the challenges for this Valuations department, apart from meeting regulatory cut off times during the day for fund valuation, is to source prices for all of the securities in the portfolio. In order to do this, they will use a number of different sources such as Bloomberg, Reuters, Datastream and FT Extel.

Reporting derivatives positions in valuations can be particularly troublesome, since it requires an offsetting item for the derivative itself. If a fund manager has an open futures position giving him £2,000,000 worth of UK equity exposure, he will only have paid a relatively small amount out of the fund (the 'margin[32]') eg £50,000. Unless the Valuations team insert a balancing entry (often referred to as a 'cash backing' entry), the fund will be overstated by the amount of the derivative less the margin payment.

Income

As can be imagined, asset managers will have a huge amount of income expected from coupons, dividends, maturities etc. The role of the Income department is to ensure that this income is actually received by the fund and correctly recorded for taxation calculation purposes.

Corporate Actions

In addition to Income from securities held, asset managers are involved in a great deal of corporate action activity on behalf of their clients, including rights issues, stock splits, scrip issues, IPOs etc. The role of the Corporate Actions department is to ensure that all of the necessary paperwork is completed, eg rights issues documents completed by the fund manager, handling of application forms and notification of allocation papers for IPOs etc.

In addition, the Corporate Actions team must liaise very closely with the Valuations team to ensure that new security lines such as IPOs and rights issues are correctly accounted for in published valuations (eg some IPOs must be reported in the fund valuation at their purchase price, until they start trading on the open market).

Investment Accounting

The Investment Accounting team are responsible for maintaining the asset manager's 'prime record' of the holdings of the client's fund. This includes recording all purchases and sales, and also any interest accruals, capital gains tax liabilities, dividend entitlements etc. for the fund. This data is used for a number of purposes, not least of which is to provide the base data for the Valuations team. Transactions are recorded on specific systems designed for asset managers.

One of the conventions used is to record and report transactions on an 'exposure' rather than a 'settled' basis. This means that if a fund manager buys a UK equity today, the investment accounting system will show this

---

[32] Margin is the term given to payments made to derivatives exchanges against potential future losses on positions taken.

security in his holdings immediately, even though the security has not yet been paid for.

Custodial Reconciliation

As mentioned above, a separate bank will act as custodian for the client, looking after the physical securities and cash on his behalf. A key function is ensuring that the asset manager's records are in line with the actual positions at custodian, this being performed by the Custodial Reconciliation (or 'Recs') section.

Retail Administration

Under unitized vehicle regulations, asset managers providing unitized products must maintain records of unit holdings by the investing public in OEICs etc. This is carried out by the asset manager's back office, who are usually notified by Independent Financial Advisers (IFAs) who are the direct sellers of OEIC products to the general public.

Bonds

At the top level, ie where asset allocators are deciding whether to allocate funds to equities, bonds, property or cash, these asset classes are essentially 'in competition' for capital allocations. A recent example was the Fed's surprise interest rate drop in January 2001; although both bonds and equities benefited from this fall, the consensus was that the news was better for equities, leading investors to invest more in equities and thereby increase market values still further.

Within the bond market itself, allocation occurs according to the following market segments.

Market Segment	Key Economic Data
Currency of Denomination	Domestic interest rates for currency Balance of payments Long term inflation prospects
Gilts/Non Gilts	Yield spread (and history thereof) between two markets[33] Yield levels (higher yields increase corporate default risk) Current issuance from sectors/companies (eg telecoms)
Yield Curve (aka 'Maturity Buckets')	Prospective yield curve changes, caused by, eg, market demand/supply in each bucket Inflation risk premium changes (at longer end)

Property

As with all asset classes, the property market competes for allocation. Investment in property can be seen as being analogous to bond investment. A capital amount is paid out (the purchase price) in exchange for a stream of periodic (rental income) and capital repayment (sale proceeds) cash flows. In comparing this type of investment with others, fund managers need to factor in the risks and administration costs involved. Fundamental economic factors affecting property investment include demand factors (supply tends to be relatively inflexible, but remains a factor), legislative changes (eg improved tenant's rights) and Government activity (eg a drive to house the homeless).

Cash

The 'cash' asset class, eg money market instruments such as Treasury Bills and bank deposits, generally offers a lower return, through interest paid, but with the chief benefit that capital is available at short notice for investment in asset classes that asset allocators feel are 'at the bottom'.

---

[33] Analysts may well look at trends in this relationship using technical analysis techniques such as moving averages etc.

An increase in interest rates will, therefore, tend to result in an increased allocation to cash. This is for the joint reasons that interest rate rises generally depress equities, bonds and property due to the lower value of discounted cash flows, and that higher rates are available from cash instruments.

Currency

Currency investment is carried out by some asset management houses as an 'overlay' activity. This is where the overlay manager will take an independent view on the currency risk profile of the fund (eg he may feel that, although prospects for Japanese equities and/or bonds may be good, the yen will depreciate against a reference currency (usually the US dollar)).

The main factors driving currency allocations are as follows.

Factor	Impact
Interest Rates	Higher interest rates lead to appreciating currencies (due to covered interest arbitrage rule)
Factor	Impact
Demand/Supply	Higher demand leads to stronger currency (eg US dollar's role as the world's reference currency since 1971 has resulted in high demand and consequent relative strength) Indicators include trade and current account and capital investment flows
Inflation	Erodes long term currency value (through PPP)

Consistency of Returns

A key objective of asset managers is to provide *consistent* returns. Although high returns are obviously desirable, pension fund trustees would become concerned if fluctuations in the overall returns generated by fund managers became marked, even if the overall long-term fund return increased. The simple reasoning behind this is that any fluctuation represents risk (in the form of variance). This is particularly important where a fund is being used to provide cash flows for a liability stream, since it is important to be able to guarantee payments when they are required, especially with recent legislation such as the Minimum Funding Requirement (MFR).

One measure of a fund's overall risk, which will provide the fund manager with a single, understandable metric, is Value at Risk (VaR) which in simple terms is the maximum value that the fund can lose in a period, given historical market movements and using confidence interval such as 95%. Fund managers can monitor their VaR, and also use it to model different asset allocation strategies to assess their relative riskiness.

Financial Forecasting

If it is given that these economic factors (or 'inputs') drive changes to the markets in which they invest, asset managers need to transform these inputs into usable data for asset allocation decision making. The most useful information is forecasted returns for the forthcoming investment horizon for which investment decisions are being made.

One of the key inputs to portfolio construction is the expected return for different scenarios. In recent years, the forecasting of future security and market returns has been the subject of considerable research resulting in the development of new statistical techniques designed to enable market participants to better forecast the next value in an economic time-series. These techniques have been developed in response to new thinking with regard to the behaviour of financial markets.

The science of economics is fairly unique in that regulators, analysts and investors in financial markets are not independent observers of the market. Their expectations and behaviour influence the market considerably. A simple example is where buyers of large equity positions will sometimes see these positions appreciate in value very quickly simply because of the herd instinct, or because their demand squeezes liquidity and therefore increases the asset's price. More complex are situations where so-called 'moral hazard' situations are created when governments or central banks essentially (but not explicitly) underwrite borrowers. If borrowers are bailed out, they are encouraged to take more risk in the future. Other examples of systemic distortions of markets have been seen in the Economic and

Monetary Union debacle of 1992 (currency markets, particularly sterling/ dollar), the Asian financial crisis fuelled originally by banks leveraging their books based on overpriced property holdings (equities) and the Savings and Loans crisis in the US, similarly rooted in overpriced property holdings (credit markets).

Given the very significant impact of government etc behaviour on financial markets, modern statistical techniques, *inter alia*, allow for the incorporation of policy factors into econometric models. These new techniques include 'switch' type devices; depending upon whether a policy is in place (eg 'a low inflation at all costs' policy) then other factors will be more or less important. A recent example was seen in the autumn of 2000 where the UK government's policy of heavily taxing petrol meant that the barrel price of oil became a much greater influence on the economy than it would otherwise have been. Other examples might be where governments have published target zones for currencies, interest rates or inflation. The existence of these targets will provide incentives to speculators to try to push currencies outside these target ranges, for example, knowing that the government will buy (or sell) to get them back into this zone. Here government policy results in greater importance being attached to the current level of a currency etc, particularly when it starts to move towards the edge of a target zone (since it is thus cheaper and less risky for speculators to push the currency out).

The main point here is that the accurate forecasting of future values of a time series (the expected returns used earlier to calculate optimal portfolios) is an exceptionally complex field. A huge amount of work has been carried out by econometric researchers trying to develop models that are capable of forecasting with any degree of accuracy the future values of financial time series given certain economic scenarios. Appendix X gives a very high level overview of these new techniques.

CHAPTER 11

Quantitative Analysis

Introduction

Within the asset management world, quantitative analysis or 'quants' involves analysing the returns, risks and characteristics of securities, markets and portfolios. As one might imagine, this is a hugely complex and demanding field, not least because of the huge amounts of accurate data that is required to provide performance and risk analyses. Quants teams not only provide data for internal management purposes (eg to reward high risk-adjusted returns and monitor overall risk) but also for external consumption. This includes analyses for the fund's Trustees and clients on each fund's performance, turnover and risk. It is obviously absolutely key that the figures produced are of the highest possible accuracy, otherwise the asset management firm could be liable to FSA sanction for misrepresentation.

Because of the requirement for accuracy and the complex tasks involved, quants staff are often qualified to actuarial standard.

Performance analysis

Performance analysis basically falls into two categories: return calculations and performance attribution. Performance return calculations measure the change in the value of the client's investment over the measurement period attributable to the fund manager's actions. Attribution takes performance analysis to a more detailed level and seeks to explain the performance of the fund manager by analysing the fund's return and breaking it down into different risk categories impacting the fund (ie according to the 'attributes' of securities, such as currency of denomination). Thus performance return calculation tells us *what* the performance was, whilst performance attribution analysis tells us *why* the figures were good or bad.

Performance Returns

The return calculation is fairly straightforward. It is, however, important to ensure that the figure calculated reflects the fund manager's decision making and judgement, and not external events beyond his control. In general, changes to the portfolio's value can occur for the following reasons.

Change	Source of Change	Fund Manager Action?
Price of Securities in Fund	Market forces	Yes
Dividends	Security Holding	Yes
Coupon	Security Holding	Yes
Rights Issue	Security Holding	Yes
Scrip Issue	Security Holding	Yes
Capital Inflow/Outflow	Client Decision	No
Fund Management Charges	Asset Manager	No

In order fairly to assess the fund manager's performance, it is obviously important to ensure that items not under his control are excluded from the performance return. Thus a huge capital inflow should have no effect on the performance figures reported. More subtle refinements to the measurement of returns, such as attempting to eliminate the effects of the timing of a particular cash flow, are covered later.

How can one assess whether a fund's return is good, bad or indifferent? The first step is to compare the fund's return to that of its benchmark. The fund's benchmark's performance is generally calculated from changes in the values of the indices underlying the benchmark. Ideally, these indices would be provided at stock level in order to give the greatest flexibility in performance reporting; however, data is not always available to this level of granularity. In order to calculate the benchmark's return, two elements usually need to be combined, these being the top level benchmark 'split' and the percentage change in the underlying indices.

Let's assume that a benchmark has been set by the trustees to be 75% equities and 25% bonds, and the underlying indices were specified as being the MSCI World index to represent equities and the J P Morgan Government Bond index to represent bonds. The benchmark performance for a single period (usually corresponding to the frequency with which benchmark/index data is published) would be calculated in the following way (sample figures).

Index	Index Weight (from 'split')	Index Level Start	Index Level End	Index Level	Bench Return
MSCI World	75%	300.00	330.00	10%	7.5%
J P Morgan Govt Bond	25%	240.00	208.00	–15%	–3.75%
Total	100%				3.75%

If performance is required for more than one period, the returns for each period can be 'chain-linked' using the standard geometric calculation:

$$\text{Return}_{overall\_Period} = [(1 + \text{return}_{sub\_period\_1}) \times (1 + \text{return}_{sub\_period\_2}) \times \ldots \text{etc}] - 1$$

This data can then be used to calculate the relative performance of the fund against the benchmark. The calculation of the fund's performance needs to take account of those items (these manifesting themselves in the form of transactions) that are not under the control of the fund manager. In order to achieve this, the Modified Dietz return calculation is generally used:

$$\text{Return}_{t=0,t=1} = \frac{\text{FundValue}_{t=1} + \text{Income} - \text{Cashflow} - \text{FundValue}_{t=0}}{\text{FundValue}_{t=0}}$$

A general time period is used, since this calculation can be used for any periodicity (eg daily, monthly etc) and then chain-linked as above. We can now calculate the relative return of the fund to its benchmark (generally simply by subtracting the benchmark performance from the fund performance), which gives a measure of how well the fund manager has done. Appendix IX contains a detailed example of the calculation of a fund's return.

Performance Attribution

Having calculated the return of the fund, the next level of detail normally required by fund managers, Trustees and increasingly clients, is a breakdown of the sources of the performance of the fund. Attribution essentially provides an analysis of what fund managers (and/or the asset manager's investment analysts) are relatively good at, ie which influences on his fund he is good at forecasting. We should be able to see whether, for example, an equity fund manager's relative returns come mainly from selecting the best performing markets (eg UK rather than US equities), or whether they come from picking the best performing stocks (eg choosing British Telecom rather than Vodafone within the telecoms sector).

Since there are a large number of different influences on the value of a portfolio, attribution can be carried out in an enormous variety of ways. It is important that attribution is carried out in the way that decisions regarding investment in the fund are carried out. If attribution is carried out in some other way, the results will be at best meaningless and at worst very misleading.

For now, however, we will assume that decisions are made for equities using a top down process:

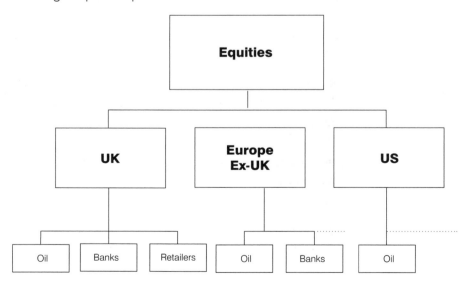

and for bonds along the following lines:

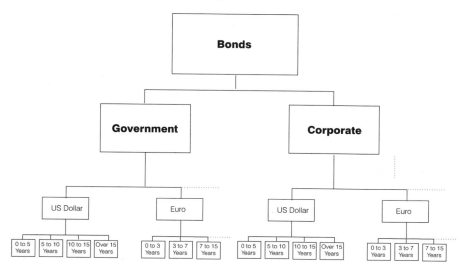

Since the hierarchies for equities and bonds are different (and in practice will normally have different decision makers) it is useful to break portfolios down into segments (or 'carve-outs' in AIMR[34] terms) in order that *relevant* influences on the portfolio (ie along the lines of the asset allocation decision making process) can be clearly analysed. Essentially, attribution analysis breaks the portfolio's relative return down into decision types such as market and industry allocation and stock selection.

Given that the above diagram is a representation of the process by which equity investment decisions are made, attribution analysis can be carried out in the following way (more detailed definitions are provided for reference in Appendix IX):

1. Calculate the weights that each stock and sector represent in the fund and benchmark

2. Calculate the return on the fund at stock level

3. Calculate the returns of each sector using appropriate indices (eg S&P 500 for US equities, 'FT Actuaries–Retailers' for UK retailers)

[34] AIMR – the Association for Investment Management and Research who have laid down standards for performance presentation.

4. Calculate the relative position taken by the fund manager, using the weights from (1) above

5. Multiply the relative weight allocated by the performance of a sector to give attribution to that sector

6. Multiply the fund weight in each sector by the fund return less the benchmark return for that sector to give attribution to overall stock selection

Other factors such as interaction between attributes, dealing timing etc are caused by events such as cash flows and trading. Attribution analysis is also complicated by the fact that the weights invested change intra month.

It is important to note, however that the analysis only provides meaningful feedback if it reflects the actual decision making process (although the information may be useful for future investment decision making). If, for example, there were no conscious and specific allocation to industry groups (instead the industry weights might simply be a by-product of stock selection), attribution to industry grouping would not provide meaningful feedback as to the effectiveness of decision making.

Fixed Interest Performance Analysis
Fixed interest return calculation and attribution is carried out in much the same way, but naturally using attributes relevant to fixed interest investment, such as yield curve allocation (ie maturity 'bucket'). Fund managers can also take an overall long position against the benchmark (this being rare in equity analysis, due to restrictions on leveraged portfolios), the effect of which can be calculated. Since fixed interest portfolios are constantly changing, attribution analysis is only really meaningful for the length of time that a strategy (or 'trade') is in place. These trades are generally in place for fairly short periods (such as a number of weeks).

Other Issues Surrounding Performance Reporting
Industry **B**est **P**ractice
Strange as it may seem, this key process does not have definitive guidelines, perhaps due to the complexities of calculation, and the difficulties encountered in sifting data. The UK's National Association of

Pension Funds (NAPF) and the US's AIMR have both laid down guidelines, but there is no particular onus on asset management companies to implement these recommendations.

Ensuring that the Analysis is Meaningful
As mentioned above, it is essential that fund performance provides a fair reflection of the value added at each stage of the investment process. In order to do this there are a number of important (and often, unfortunately, rather complex) issues to resolve. Some of the major issues are summarized below.

Return Calculation Approach
The approach of taking daily valuations and chain linking them to produce an overall period return may, at first, seem excessive. For example, the AIMR recommends that valuations only need to be taken where there is a 'significant cashflow'. The main issue surrounds the general requirement for computerized systems to have a hard and fast set of rules, thereby making it problematic for them to decide that a cash flow is 'significant'. In any event it is generally more straightforward for computer systems to take a valuation each day, rather than take valuations based on a set of rules.

Data Issues
The bane of quantitative analysts' lives lies in the sourcing and preparation of the data required to carry out performance analysis. Problems include the following:

▶ non-availability of the correct level of transaction data, eg income entitlements and receipts being linked to underlying securities.

▶ benchmark adjustments, such as those required to maintain benchmark positions within fixed 'top level' percentage splits and adjusting calculated benchmark positions back to published figures from indexed estimates

▶ Having to adjust for published performance figures, ie where performance figures have been released, and are subsequently found to be incorrect

Other Analyses

Risk Analysis

While performance is an extremely important metric, both from an external reporting and a fund management feedback perspective, there is an increasing requirement for risk analysis to be available. This is from the point of view of current risk (as expressed by, for example, a Value at Risk measure), historical risk (tracking error) and forward looking (eg by modelling the risk of prospective shifts in allocations). The 'risk' is obviously the risk of a significant downside loss to the fund; however, any period of high variance (including a sharp upswing), especially when high relative to the fund's benchmark, will increase the perceived riskiness of the fund.

The role of the Quants desk will be to calculate the volatilities of the different risks of the fund, eg currencies, equity markets and/or industry groupings, and produce analyses such as covariance matrices. The idea of these is to enable fund managers or investment analysts to identify areas where higher expected returns can be obtained for the same level of risk, or where the same expected overall portfolio returns can be obtained for a lower risk level.

Other Areas

Due to their quantitative skill set, Quants teams are also often responsible for running index-tracking funds, which requires that they match the index as closely as they can with fewer stocks than the number of which the index is comprised; this can be achieved through the calculation of the fund's historic and prospective tracking error. In addition they may get involved in the forecasting of market returns, using the increasingly sophisticated econometric and other tools now available, for use in asset allocation decision making by investment directors.

CHAPTER 12

Compliance

Introduction

Asset managers are responsible not only for the professional and responsible investment of their clients' funds, but also for the correct and accurate reporting of transactions carried out, fund valuation and performance. They must also ensure the safekeeping of the clients' assets, generally by making arrangements with a custodian bank specializing in this type of service. Although the requirements of compliance with UK investment regulations are onerous, the tight regulation of UK investment business is a cornerstone of the continuing success of the UK asset management industry.

The regulations that apply to asset managers are summarized below. All staff responsible for the management of clients' funds are required to know and understand these rules. Trainee fund managers are required to pass the Investment Management Certificate (IMC), a large part of which focuses on compliance rules, before being allowed formally to make and/ or implement investment decisions on a client's behalf. This qualification is run by the UK Society of Investment Professionals (UKSIP) on behalf of the regulatory bodies.

UK asset management companies are regulated by the Financial Services Authority (FSA) which is a legal body with statutory powers granted under the Financial Services and Markets Act 2000 (FSMA 2000). The FSA is a company limited by guarantee, where this guarantee is made by HM Treasury.

The regulatory regime is designed to protect the interests of the private investor by imposing stringent regulations upon companies engaging in asset management (and other investment businesses). It is a criminal offence to provide asset management services without the FSA's authorization punishable by up to 2 years imprisonment plus an unlimited fine.

The following is a summary of those conduct of business guidelines specifically applying to asset managers. These guidelines are designed to ensure that asset management firms and their staff are 'fit and proper' to manage investors' (and in particular private investors') money. The guidelines are known as the FSA's eleven 'Principles of Business' and are summarized below:

1. Integrity – making profits fairly

2. Relations with Regulators – adopting an open and cooperative approach

3. Customers' Assets – adequate arrangements must be made for the safekeeping (custody) of clients' assets

4. Customer Communications – clients informational needs must be met as far as possible

5. Skill, care and diligence – work must be carried out to a high standard

6. Customers' interests – firms must always act with their clients' best interests at heart

7. Market conduct – firms must adhere to 'proper' standards of behaviour

8. Management and control systems – eg having adequate risk control systems

9. Financial prudence – having adequate resources to meet clients' requirements

10. Customer: Relationship of Trust – ensuring that products offered to clients are appropriate to their needs

11. Conflicts of interest – must be handled fairly by firms

In addition to these client-specific rules, asset management firms are obliged to play their part in ensuring that illegal activities such as insider dealing and money laundering do not occur.

If the FSA feels that firms are in breach of these guidelines they have the ultimate sanction of withdrawing a firm's authorization thereby making it illegal for them to continue to trade.

Compliance Rule Summary

Most of the rules that asset managers must abide by are common sense. The rules revolve around acting in the client's best interests, putting your client's interests before your own, as well as ensuring that the firm's actions do not break any UK laws.

Disclosure of Major Share Interests

In order to ensure that the stock market is fair to all investors, any situation where a single investor (or a group of investors acting together – this being known as a concert party) can exert undue influence over a public company through the size of its shareholding must be reported. The Companies Act requires that any investor, or group of investors acting together, owning 3% or more of the issued share capital of a company must declare their holding. Further, any *change* to holdings falling into this category of 1% or more must also be reported.

Conflict of Interest

Owning Own Corporation's Shares

These days most asset managers are part of larger banking groups. There is a clear potential conflict of interest in investing clients' money in shares of your own company.

Own Account Trading

Since fund managers are controlling large amounts of capital, they can clearly influence share prices through the purchase or sale of large quantities of a particular security. For this reason they are required to declare any positions that they are holding, either within a company's own 'book' or within the fund manager's own personal position. Fund managers are obliged to report these positions (and any trading) to their firm's compliance department, who will also monitor the company's own book. They are also required to execute any client trades before they deal on their own behalf, except where it would clearly be in the client's interests for trading to be carried out after own account trading.

Acting in the Client's Best Interests

Inducements

Both individual fund managers and asset management firms as a whole are restricted in the types of inducements that they are allowed to accept from brokers looking for the fund manager to place orders for securities through them. In general, brokers fall into two categories: those providing background research into securities that fund managers may wish to buy and those not providing this research, but instead paying an amount of 'soft commission'. Under the regulations, this soft commission can only be spent by the fund management organization on data and systems which assist it in the making of investment decisions. Thus, fund managers can use this money to pay for research systems such as Datastream and Bloomberg, but may not use it to buy general accounting or personnel system software.

Gifts from brokers to fund manager also need to be kept under control. Any substantial gift must be reported to the asset management company's compliance department, who will decide whether the gift can be accepted.

Churning the Account

This particularly applies to fund managers who earn all or part of the fees based on the volume of market trades carried out on the client's account. Fund managers are not allowed to generate an excessive number of transactions even if the trades are in the client's interests.

Best Execution

An asset management company is obliged to obtain for his clients the best price in the market when carrying out trades on a fund's behalf. Thus, the executive carrying out any trade has to get a series of quotes from different brokers and is obliged to 'hit' the lowest quote if buying, and the highest quote if selling.

Dealing on Behalf of a Group of Clients

The fund manager must be seen to be treating all clients equally at all times, which mainly implies that clients with similar investment objectives should be invested in the same securities, and that when buying and selling in the market all clients should get the same price. Fund managers will, therefore, generally generate orders for multiple clients at one time. This practice also enables them to obtain better prices for securities bought and sold, as well as minimizing administration costs. This obligation flows through to other scenarios in which fund managers take advantage of the availability of a tranche of securities (usually equities) at an unusually low price. Here the fund manager must fairly allocate these securities across his clients. The same would apply to any Initial Public Offerings (IPOs) in which a fund manager is participating.

'Fit and Proper'

The asset management company is obliged to ensure that its systems and staff are capable of efficiently running the clients' funds. This implies that all staff are properly trained, and the supervisors have the necessary level of experience to carry out their respective roles within the firm. As mentioned above, investment staff must have the qualifications required to demonstrate that they know and understand what is required of them in their dealings on behalf of their clients. This 'threshold competency' requirement means that fund managers must have passed the IMC, and preferably have passed all of the UKSIP's associateship examinations. In addition, all other staff carrying out support functions, such as dealing, back office settlement, corporate actions and reconciliations, must have the required level of knowledge and, where required, qualifications to carry out their duties to a reasonable standard.

Risks

Asset management houses are required to ensure that their clients are kept fully informed with regard to the risks that they are taking. The letter of the regulation actually states that this dialogue should be occurring every time that a transaction is carried out for the customer. This may be difficult to comply with in practice; however, the fund manager should be able to provide periodic and ad-hoc risk reporting in order that the client can understand the level of risk incurred.

Legal Compliance

In addition to compliance with the regulations of financial self-regulatory bodies, UK asset management companies are also obliged to observe UK law. One of the main requirements concerns money laundering, where asset management companies must ensure that they are not assisting criminals to 'legitimize' money derived from activities including terrorism and drug-trafficking. In addition, fund managers must not act upon any 'insider' knowledge. This is information obtained from individuals with access to price-sensitive information obtained within a quoted company, but which has not been released to the general share-buying public.

Investment Powers

Asset managers generally run their clients' funds on a 'discretionary' basis, ie they can use their own skill and judgement to make investment decisions on the client's behalf, without constant reference to their client. These powers are, however, constrained by the fund manager's obligations with respect to the objectives of the fund (eg delivering the cash flows required to meet pension fund payment stream liabilities) and any restrictions on the types of investment (eg investments perceived as being 'unethical' by the client). Most fund's interests are owned by more than one person (these being known as 'pooled' funds such as unitized vehicles or pension or life funds). Normally a Trustee will be appointed to monitor the fund, who will require reports enabling him to check that the guidelines for the management of the fund are being observed. For pension funds, Trustees are responsible for ensuring that guidelines such as the Minimum Funding Requirement (MFR) regulations are observed, ie that the pension fund will be able to provide holders of a defined benefit pension scheme with their expected pension income.

Investment restrictions constraining investment carried out on behalf of funds fall into two main categories, those prevailing because of the type of fund (eg unitized vehicle rules) and those put in place by particular clients. Included in the types of restriction in place for unitized vehicles is the constraint that the fund cannot invest more than 5% in one security (since one of the purposes of unitized vehicles such as OEICS is to give investors an opportunity to diversify their risk across a larger number of securities than they would otherwise be able to). It must also limit the exposure of the fund to 'unquoted securities' as a group to no more than 10% of its overall value (since these are seen as risky investments). As a direct result of the Peter Young scandal (see below) the regulations extend this 10% limit to 'pre-listed' shares, which are shares that are 'just about' to be listed.

Additionally it cannot hold more than 10% of the issued share capital of any company (in order that the risk of the company invested in is spread across investors). Another rule is that the fund cannot go overdrawn. This is partially to prevent the fund from becoming leveraged, which is seen as being too risky, and partially to avoid the cost of borrowing to the fund.

Other types of restrictions are specified by clients and/or their trustees. These can include prohibiting fund investment in companies perceived by the client to be engaged in unethical businesses such as tobacco or arms manufacture. Pension fund Trustees usually disallow investment in 'risky' asset types such as derivatives.

Case Study: Peter Young – What Went Wrong?

Background

One of the highest profile cases involving the breach of compliance rules by a fund manager (rather than the rather more commonplace cases involving mis-selling of pensions and other investment products) was that of Peter Young, who was a European Fund Manager at Morgan Grenfell Asset Management (MGAM). MGAM, which was owned by the giant Frankfurt-based Deutsche Bank, was a successful manager of unit trusts whose performance record had attracted a large number of investors in its funds. Young himself was responsible for over £1.4 billion of clients' money.

In October 1998 Young, an Oxford maths graduate and former star fund manager, was charged by the Serious Fraud Office with conspiracy to defraud and other serious offences under the Financial Services Act (1986). His actions resulted in his parent company having to pay over £400,000,000 in compensation to investors, the dismissal of six senior investment management company executives, the heavy fining of the fund's trustees and the eventual disappearance of the name of his company from the financial world.

The facts of the case are now fairly well established. Young had built up very large positions in unquoted companies which were operating in high-risk businesses, often outside the fund's intended European geographical zone. These securities were classified (by Young himself) as 'pre-listed' securities, thereby circumventing strict SIB rules regarding a fund's percentage exposure to unquoted (and therefore more risky) securities. As the scandal unravelled, it became clear that at least one of the companies invested in by Young had channelled funds directly to Young himself in the form of an uncollateralized 'loan' for his new luxury house in Buckinghamshire. A significant proportion of the 'companies' held in Young's funds were in actuality no more than Luxembourg-based shells (usually referred to as 'letter-box' companies since there is little more to them than a business address).

IMRO investigators also found that the management of MGAM had not established adequate controls, nor had they followed up on early warnings that problems might exist. Instead they continued to give free rein to their star fund manager. In early 1996, at a time when his fund was clearly in breach of an IMRO guideline, Young was paid a £235,000 bonus and promoted to the board of MGAM.

The extent of the damage was enormous; the funds involved were found to have over £220,000,000 missing, with a further estimated £180,000,000 being wiped off the fund due to the adverse publicity caused. The affair caused shockwaves to reverberate around the investment world, particularly in the unit trust market, which saw a dramatic slowdown in the numbers of units sold. Deutsche Bank injected over £400 million into the fund to keep it going and shortly afterwards dropped the name Morgan Grenfell, which had been one of the UK's foremost merchant banks, from nearly all of its companies.

What Went Wrong?

One of the most worrying facets of this case was the failure of so many participants to carry out their roles effectively. Even when breaches of regulations were discovered, no effective action was taken. Indeed MGAM continued to market these funds aggressively even when they were clearly misrepresenting their true nature (eg presenting them as European funds, when a significant proportion of the fund's capital was invested outside most people's definition of 'Europe').

To summarize the roles of the respective participants, and their actual behaviour:

Participant	Responsibility	Actual Behaviour
Fund Manager	Safe investment of clients' money in sound European securities with an acceptable risk profile	Investment of funds in extremely high risk ventures, not always in Europe. Channelling of funds for his own personal use.
Compliance Officer	Ensure that detected breaches of regulations are quickly rectified	Allowed positions to go further outside regulation limits, for many months after initial detection
MGAM Directors	Take decisive action when rules were breached. Create a culture of teamwork and collective responsibility. Ensure that data and records are maintained by independent sources	Allowed positions to continue to break limits. Created a 'star fund manager', who could override all other staff members. Allowed fund manager to price and classify his positions as he wished
Trustees	Ensure that fund remains within the limits of its specific mandate and of any regulations pertaining to the type of fund	Failed on all counts to check actual holdings and positions against the mandate
Brokers	Inform Directors that a position representing an unacceptably large percentage of the capitalization of a security has been built up	Did not inform MGAM directors
MGAM Marketing	Provide investors with accurate information with regard to the risks of the funds	Continued to market the funds as before

The causes of the problem, while all falling under the general rubric of 'non-compliance', can be categorized as follows. Criminal action, eg using clients' funds for one's own purposes. Cultural issues, mainly the all-important 'star fund manager' approach. Finally the lack of effective, independent systems which could have flagged up the full nature of the positions built up.

In an IMRO statement, the regulator was quoted as saying 'It was reported to at least one member of the board of Morgan Grenfell Asset Management, by no later than April, 1996, that the fund manager persistently acted in a way that abided by the letter rather than the spirit of the unit trust regulations, despite giving several undertakings to change his behaviour. The irregularities were connected with – although not limited to – Peter Young, who carried out day-to-day management of European Growth and Capital Growth.'

This case highlights the importance of obeying not just the letter of the regulations. It is very important having the necessary systems, data management procedures and risk management controls in place. Additionally, the dangers of giving too much control to one individual (which echoes the Leeson–Barings case) are clear. The bottom line is that there isn't really a totally prescriptive list of do's and don'ts for asset managers. It is the responsibility of the firm's management to ensure not only the existence of effective procedures, systems and controls but also that a spirit of collective responsibility prevails in the company to ensure that the regulatory, legal and client requirements are met.

CHAPTER 13

Systems and Data Requirements

Introduction

As in many industries, technology is playing an increasing role in all
aspects of asset management, from security and market analysis through
fund position monitoring to deal processing and fund pricing. The main
information technology (IT) tools in general use, which are either
developed by the fund manager's IT departments or bought 'off-the-shelf'
from specialist software houses, can be categorized as follows.

Tool	Example Systems/Suppliers	Deployment
Real Time Data feeds	Bloomberg Reuters	▶ Real time news for fund managers ▶ Up to data price guides for dealers
News servers	Multex Reuters Bloomberg	▶ Ability to search for historical news stories relating to particular markets/companies ▶ Fund manager alerted to relevant news stories
Security Analysis	Datastream FactSet	▶ Historical analysis of securities ▶ Company account

Tool	Example Systems/Suppliers	Deployment
Portfolio Analysis	Primark PreView DST Open Front Office Shadow In-house Development	▶ Fund position vs benchmark reporting ▶ Breakdown of fund using required classifications (eg company size, credit rating etc)
Portfolio Rebalancing	DST Open Orders In-house development	▶ Calculation of orders required to move portfolios into line with the fund manager's 'model' position
Order Management and Dealing	Landmark DST Open Orders Charles Rivers In-house Development	▶ Pre-trade compliance checking (ie will a proposed order break a restriction?) ▶ Routing of fund manager orders to dealers for market execution ▶ Recording of market trades ▶ Routing of executed orders to the back office settlement team
Electronic Settlement	In-house Development	▶ Automatic confirmation of market trade against broker 'allegation' ▶ Exception reporting of mismatches

Tool	Example Systems/Suppliers	Deployment
Investment Accounting	Hi-Portfolio FMC Datastream Bureau	▶ Recording of all fund activity (buys, sells, cash injections, dividends, coupons, corporate actions etc) ▶ Reporting tools (eg formal valuations, transaction reporting) ▶ Calculation of accruals, entitlements etc
Unit Pricing System	In-house Development	Calculate market price for in-house unitized vehicles (up to four times per day)
Reconciliation	In-house Development	Reconciliation of asset manager's investment accounting system with custodial records

These systems are very specific to the asset management industry, and are characterized by their voracious appetite for accurate data. Indeed, even within the asset management company itself, the systems and data required are very specific to each department.

Desk Specific Requirements

Fund Managers

Fund managers and analysts are basically interested in any and all information that will affect the values of their portfolios. Although they are mainly focused on the long-term investment horizon, many active managers use real-time news and data services to monitor changes in market conditions, with a view to switching between securities to take advantage of perceived opportunities. Traditionally, the fund manager's main guide to his position has been his valuation report, which might display his current holdings in nominal, value and percentage terms. As technology advances, and data suppliers become increasingly able to provide key data such as index constituents and their weightings, fund manager tools are becoming increasingly sophisticated.

Portfolio Rebalancing

Fund managers are principally interested in the securities that they are currently holding, and in securities which are constituents of indices not currently held, but against which the fund manager is measured. This holdings data can be presented in a number of ways (eg nominal shares held or value of holdings in base or local currency), but the most useful for portfolio modelling are the percentages of the fund that each holding represents. In addition, the data is generally grouped using security classifications such as market or industry in order that a fund manager can look at his composite holdings in industrial sectors. An example section of a UK equity fund report might look like this.

	Fund %	Benchmark %
Oils	3.3	4.6
BG Group		0.8
Enterprise	1.2	1.0
Shell	3.1	2.8
Chemicals	2.5	3.4
BOC	2.5	2.3
Croda		1.1
Pharms	12.1	10.2
Astrazeneca	3.9	3.1

Thus the fund manager can see both where he is and is not invested in particular stocks, and also where he is over- or underweight with respect to the index for industries and/or stocks. The amount of effort required in order to provide this type of analysis should not be underestimated. In addition to the initial system set up, the ongoing maintenance of the data, in terms of ensuring that fund positions are correct, and that benchmark data is up to date, is considerable.

This analysis can be taken to the next logical stage by introducing the concept of the fund manager's ideal, or 'model', percentage position for each security (and therefore for each industry grouping). This is usually expressed in terms of a percentage 'bet' against the benchmark position (thus if a fund manager doesn't want to hold an index constituent in his portfolio, he will effectively have a negative bet being the equal and opposite of the benchmark weight, eg:

	Fund %	Benchmark %	'Bet' %	Model %
Oils	3.3	4.6	0.0	3.3
BG Group		0.8	−0.8	0.0
Enterprise	1.2	1.0	0.5	1.5
Shell	3.1	2.8	0.3	3.1
Chemicals	2.5	3.4	−0.6	2.5
BOC	2.5	2.3	0.5	2.8
Croda		1.1	−1.1	0.0
Pharms	12.1	10.2	0.6	11.9
Astrazeneca	3.9	3.1	0.6	3.7

The percentage rebalancing action required to bring the portfolio in line with the fund manager's mode is calculated by subtracting the fund's current position from the model percentage. This percentage can be used to calculate the value of equity to be bought by multiplying the total fund value by this percentage; then dividing this amount by the current market price of the stock, the nominal number of equities to buy or sell can be calculated.

Total Fund Value: £226,363,951

	Fund %	Model %	Rebalancing %	Rebalancing Amount (£)	Security Price	Nominal to to Buy/Sell
Oils	3.3	3.3				
BG Group		0.0	0.0	0	281p	0
Enterprise	1.2	1.5	0.3	679,091	576p	117,898
Shell	3.1	3.1	0.0	0	560p	0
Chemicals	2.5	2.5				
BOC	2.5	2.8	0.3	679,091	£10.35	656
Croda		0.0	0	0	276p	0
Pharms	12.1	11.9				
Astrazeneca	3.9	3.7	−0.2	452,728	£34.20	132

Although one could place an order in the market for exactly 117,898 shares in Enterprise Oil, one would quickly run out of friends in the brokerage business. Indeed in some markets, shares are only traded in minimum 'Board Lot Sizes' (the smallest level of granularity possible) of a given number of shares. Examples are Indonesia (500 for all stocks except banks which are 5,000), Korea (10) and Singapore (1,000). For the UK , the fund manager can generally use his discretion, taking into account the size of the funds that he is rebalancing. In this case, given that there are two securities with high prices, he might round the nominal ordered to the nearest 10 shares. This can be achieved by using simple rounding mechanisms generally available with spreadsheets and other tools.

Fund of Funds 'Look-Through' Analysis

Many funds do not themselves invest directly in underlying securities markets, but rather buy and sell units of unitized vehicles such as OEICs, which specialize in a particular area of the market. Although this is a convenient and cost-efficient way to organize global investment, it can be difficult for the overall fund manager to analyse his fund beyond the level of seeing his allocation to the unitized funds themselves. A useful device in this case is a 'look-through' routine, which calculates the implicit holding of the top level fund in securities held in the unitized vehicle. For example, let's say that a top level fund was holding units of a series of OEICs in order to gain exposure to global markets.

Global Aggressive Investor Fund

Unitized Vehicle Held	Holding	Price (£)	Value (£)
UK Equity Growth Fund	1,550,000	15.6	24,180,000
Euro Equity High Growth	1,400,000	9.42	13,188,000
US Technology Fund	1,805,000	6.48	11,696,400
Total			49,064,400

And that the OEICs themselves were invested in the following securities (numbers are limited to keep the example manageable).

UK Equity Growth Fund

Security	Holding	Price	Value (£)	Industry Group
Bass	5,339,280	751p	40,098,000	Breweries, Pubs, Restaurants
Marconi	12,647,100	717p	90,679,740	IT Hardware
Morse	5,801,480	368p	21,349,450	Software and Computer Services
Reuters	8,006,500	£11.20	89,672,810	Media
Total			241,800,000	

Euro Equity High Growth

Security	Holding	Price	Value (£)	Industry Group
Air Liquide	598,490	€159.40	66,947,030	Chemicals
Canal Studio	1,898,640	€9.95	13,257,150	Media
CAP Gemini	437,020	€168.50	51,675,820	Software and Computer Services
Total			131,880,000	

US Technology Fund

Security	Holding	Price	Value (£)	Industry Group
CISCO	1,294,770	$41.90	36,167,120	IT Hardware
Microsoft	1,277,060	$48.56	41,342,560	Software and Computer Services
Oracle	1,818,170	$32.55	39,454,320	Software and Computer Services
Total			116,964,000	

It is obviously easy enough to calculate the percentage exposure to each market, since the funds are already segregated into markets. However, the fund manager may well wish to know what his overall global exposure to technology stocks is, given that he has a high exposure to US technology stocks. In order to calculate this, the following steps need to be taken:

1. Calculate the implied position in each security by the 'top level' fund resulting from holdings in the investing funds

2. Use the security level classifications to group these securities together by industry

3. Combine the classifications 'IT Hardware' and 'Software and Computer Services' to give the overall exposure of the fund to 'Technology'

Taking these steps in turn:

Implied Positions

The implied position for each security can be calculated in a number of ways. One suggested approach, calculating the implied nominal holding in each security, is as follows;

(a) Calculate the percentage that each top level fund holding represents as a percentage of the investing fund

(b) Multiply the nominal holding in each security by the percentage calculated in (a)

In our small example, the following results would be obtained.

Global Aggressive Investor Fund

Unitized Vehicle Held	Holding	Price (£)	Value (£)	Total Value of Investing Fund	%
UK Equity Growth Fund	1,550,000	15.6	24,180,000	241,800,000	10.0
Euro Equity High Growth	1,400,000	9.42	13,188,000	131,880,000	10.0
US Technology Fund	1,805,000	6.48	11,696,400	116,964,000	10.0
Total			49,064,400		

UK Equity Growth Fund

Security	Holding	Percentage In Top-Level Fund	Implied Holding in Top-Level Fund
Bass	5,339,280	10.0	533,928
Marconi	12,647,100	10.0	1,264,710
Morse	5,801,480	10.0	580,148
Reuters	8,006,500	10.0	800,650

Euro Equity Growth Fund

Security	Holding	Percentage In Top-Level Fund	Implied Holding in Top-Level Fund
Air Liquide	598,490	10.0	59,849
Canal Studio	1,898,640	10.0	189,864
CAP Gemini	437,020	10.0	43,702

US Technology Fund

Security	Holding	Percentage In Top-Level Fund	Implied Holding in Top-Level Fund
CISCO	1,294,770	10.0	129,477
Microsoft	1,277,060	10.0	127,706
Oracle	1,818,170	10.0	181,817

A useful check at this stage is to ensure that the total of all of these implied positions adds up to the total value of the top-level fund.

Global Aggressive Investor Fund (Implied Stock Level Positions)

Security	Implied Holding in in Top-Level Fund	Price	Implied Value
Bass	533,928	751p	4,009,799
Marconi	1,264,710	717p	9,067,971
Morse	580,148	368p	2,134,945
Reuters	800,650	£11.20	8,967,280
Air Liquide	59,849	E159.40	6,694,646
Canal Studio	189,864	E9.95	1,325,709
CAP Gemini	43,702	E168.50	5,167,538
CISCO	129,477	$41.90	3,616,721
Microsoft	127,706	$48.56	4,134,265
Oracle	181,817	$32.55	3,945,425
Total			49,064,298

The very slight shortfall is not significant for our purposes here.

Group by Industrial Classification

The next step is to group the securities according to their industrial classification, effectively creating an implied pan-global industrial breakdown.

Global Aggressive Investor Fund (Implied Industry and Stock Level Positions)

Security	Implied Value	Implied %
Breweries, Pubs, Restaurants	4,009,799	8.17
Bass	4,009,799	8.17
Chemicals	6,694,646	13.64
Air Liquide	6,694,646	13.64
IT Hardware	12,684,692	25.85
CISCO	3,616,721	7.37
Marconi	9,067,971	18.48
Media	10,292,989	20.98
Canal Studio	1,325,709	2.70
Reuters	8,967,280	18.28
Software and Computer Services	15,382,173	31.35
CAP Gemini	5,167,538	10.53
Microsoft	4,134,265	8.43
Morse	2,134,945	4.35
Oracle	3,945,425	8.04
Total	49,064,298	100.00

Technology Exposure

Finally, a customized classification of 'Technology', perhaps with a corresponding 'Non-Technology' classification for the other securities needs to be established. The presentation for the fund manager might, therefore, be as follows.

Global Aggressive Investor Fund (Implied Industry and Stock Level Positions)

Security	Implied Value	Implied %
NON-TECHNOLOGY	10,704,445	21.81
Breweries, Pubs, Restaurants	*4,009,799*	*8.17*
Bass	4,009,799	8.17
Chemicals	*6,694,646*	*13.64*
Air Liquide	6,694,646	13.64
TECHNOLOGY	38,359,854	78.18
IT Hardware	*12,684,692*	*25.85*
CISCO	3,616,721	7.37
Marconi	9,067,971	18.48
Media	*10,292,989*	*20.98*
Canal Studio	1,325,709	2.70
Reuters	8,967,280	18.28
Software and Computer Services	*15,382,173*	*31.35*
CAP Gemini	5,167,538	10.53
Microsoft	4,134,265	8.43
Morse	2,134,945	4.35
Oracle	3,945,425	8.04
Total	*49,064,298*	*100.00*

Thus the fund manager can see what his exposure is to technology companies, as an implied result of his holdings in unitized vehicles.

In practice, this data would be of most use when compared to the fund manager's benchmark. Thus if the fund manager was benchmarked against the Morgan Stanley Capital International (MSCI) Global Index, the following steps would be required to provide the fund manager with his relative position analysis.

> ▶ Download the index constituent securities, including the following data:

▶ Market capitalization

▶ MSCI industrial classification

▶ Calculate the weight that each security represents of the overall index

▶ Identify the MSCI industry classifications that fall into the fund manager's interpretation of 'Technology' (and therefore 'Non-Technology')

▶ Group the securities by the qualifying classifications identified above

▶ Sum the weights of each security falling within each fund manager category to give the required analysis

All of the above functions can be relatively easily achieved using standard PC desktop tools such as Excel and Access.

Adjusting Position Data for Capital Gains Tax Liabilities

Most asset management houses use data captured in their investment accounting systems to provide fund managers with their current positions. In most instances this is fine, the main issues being the lag between dealing and position updating (since the trades need to be processed and entered into the investment accounting system) and the reconciliation between the fund manager's analysis system and the investment accounting system.

However, when carrying out the 'look-through' analysis described above, a significant distortion can occur due to the requirement for unitized vehicle pricing to include a provision for Capital Gains Tax (CGT) liabilities. This provision is calculated from the sum of the gains made on positions held within the fund, which are calculated by subtracting the book cost[35] (ie the amount that the stock cost when purchased) from the current marked-to-market value. The amount of capital gains tax liability is calculated each day, as if the fund were to be completely 'cashed in' and all gains and

---

[35] A detailed example of book cost calculation is provided in Appendix X.

losses realized. This amount is then deducted from the overall value of the fund prior to the unit price being calculated.

Although this might be seen as prudent accounting, this system will not give an accurate reflection of the amount of assets actually under management at any given time (which is irrespective of whether funds will be partially used to pay taxes). This is particularly the case when calculating the 'look-through' analysis outlined above, which is completely reliant upon having unit prices which represent the value of the positions actually held in the fund.

In order to compensate for this, the amount of the CGT liability needs to be added back into each of the funds held by the 'top level' fund, in order that the analysis correctly reflects underlying holdings.

Other Fund Manager Tools

The following is a brief resumé of some of the other fund manager tools generally used, with the main design features required.

Order Management

The main requirements of an order management system can be summarized as follows:

- Pre-trade compliance checking, ie ensuring that the fund manager would not be in breach of any regulatory or client restrictions if he went ahead with the trade (this being a requirement of increased importance after the Peter Young affair)

- Routing of orders from the fund manager (preferably directly from a rebalancing system similar to that outlined above) to the relevant dealer's desk

- Reporting on trade status, ie whether completed, warehoused, partially filled etc

Transaction Reporting

Ability to report on trades carried out on behalf of a client, giving details of the security traded, nominal, price dealt, transaction date, broker used etc. Associated analyses would include:

▶ All transactions for a given date range

▶ All transactions for a particular security

▶ Amount of business put a particular broker's way in a given time-frame, this being particularly important when trying to balance soft commission targets between brokers

Performance Reporting

The ultimate feedback tool for the fund manager is knowledge of his performance (as discussed in the 'Quants' chapter), in particular the attribution of performance to different market risks taken (eg currency, industrial sector etc).

Dealers

In addition to their real time price and news services, the main requirement for dealers is to record deals transacted with counterparties in the market. Although very little actual screen-based dealing is carried out[36] (parcels of securities tend to be too large for this), there is an increasing trend for deals to be recorded using a system, rather than being recorded on paper tickets. The benefits of this type of system to the asset management firm mainly revolve around the removal of the requirement for faxing of tickets and the subsequent retyping of deal data in the back office, with the associated risks of transcription errors. In addition it presents the opportunity for the staff with the greatest level of knowledge about the securities being traded (ie the fund managers and dealers) to capture the data electronically. This can considerably reduce errors in settlement through ensuring that security codes etc are correct.

Client Services and Marketing

In addition to applications designed to give investors on-line access to data regarding the asset manager's products (and in some cases the ability to buy and sell units held), client-facing departments have an increasing requirement to provide information to current and potential investors.

Generally, this information is provided for positions that are slightly out of

---

[36] Dealing is generally actually carried out over the phone, with all deals being recorded in paper blotters on the dealers' desks. The role of the computer system is to capture data electronically in order that it can be more easily used across the organization, and to avoid rekeying errors.

date (eg three months old) since the data is being placed in the public domain (and will, therefore, be accessible by the asset manager's competitors). The information provided includes performance data, largest holdings and percentage allocation by currency, market, industry etc.

Compliance

The compliance department need to be able to monitor all of an asset management house's positions and activity in order to ensure that regulatory and client restrictions are not being broken. The types of systems and data requirements are as follows.

Rule Type	Periodicity	System Requirement	Data Requirement
% of issued capital held	Daily (Exception Report)	▶ Calculate percentage held of all stocks across all funds/ groups of funds/ individual funds ▶ Report on positions over given percentage of issued capital	▶ Fund nominal ▶ Current price ▶ Market cap
% each stock represents in fund	Daily (Exception Report)	▶ Calculate percentage weight of each position in each unitized fund ▶ Report positions over given percentage	▶ Fund nominal ▶ Current price
Dealing	Ad-hoc	Report all trades for user selected security across given date range	Transaction data for all funds

Back Office

The requirements of back office departments such as settlements, confirmations, reconciliation, unit pricing etc may be met by the implementation of one system or platform. Some of the key requirements are as follows.

Investment Accounting

The main requirement here is that the asset management house can accurately value all of its client's portfolios. This is in order that it can provide accurate valuation data (either printed and/or electronic) for internal (eg fund manager position reporting) and external (eg client valuation reports) purposes. In order to do this the investment accounting system needs to be able to carry out the following functions:

- Calculate the client fund current positions from data entered manually or fed electronically for:

- Deals

- Corporate actions

- Fund inflows and outflows

- Price all client fund holdings, mainly by using a market price feed

- Calculate book prices and book costs

- Calculate capital gains tax liabilities

- Calculate dividend and coupon entitlements

Settlements and Confirmations

The main requirement here is the matching of the 'broker allegation', ie what the broker has executed in the market on behalf of the fund, with the asset manager's own record which has, perhaps, been captured using an order management system. The system should retain an audit trail of all matches, but only alert settlements and confirms staff to any mis-matches. The systems are usually based on standard messaging protocols (ie formats such as those established by SWIFT to facilitate communication between financial institutions).

Unitized Fund Pricing

Most unitized funds such as OEICs need to be formally priced on a daily basis, in order that the units bought by investors can be fairly priced. The pricing of units needs to be calculated from the total value of the holdings, adjusted for management charges, CGT liabilities, etc, and then divided by the number of units in issue.

Key Systems Requirements

The following is a summary of the types of features that need to be incorporated into the systems infrastructure to provide asset management staff with the analyses that they require.

Feature	Requirement Type
Database with flexible indexing	Ability to classify securities in many different ways
Time series data capability Performance analysis	▶ Historical position reporting ·
Auditability	▶ Ability to track changes to data ▶ Full audit trail of transactions carried out on client funds
Intelligent data enhancement	▶ Benchmark indexation ▶ Preferred price sourcing by security ▶ Conservative credit rating ▶ Sensibility check (eg Bond Duration $<=$ Maturity)
System Backup/Contingency	Enable business to keep running in the event of system failure/disaster

Key Data Requirements

General

Fund managers often choose to source their data from different vendors depending upon the market in which they are investing. Thus for mainstream securities they may choose to source data from exchanges (via Reuters, Bloomberg or other vendor), whereas less widely traded security data may be sourced directly from brokers specializing in those markets. It has become essential that this data is available electronically in order that it can be utilized within the fund manager's portfolio analysis systems. In order for this security data to be usable, it must be indexed by one or more recognizable and unique security code series. The main codes in use are as follows:

- Stock Exchange Daily Official List (SEDOLs), generally the code of choice for equities

- International Security Identification Number (ISINs), preferred for bonds

- Datastream, Reuters and Bloomberg have their own code series for use in their systems

- Exchange Ticker (often used by investment staff to refer to a particular security)

Since the asset management house's investment accounting system is generally its prime record of investment activity and positions for client funds, its data is generally used throughout the organization including the front office. It is important, therefore, that the requirements of the front office are taken into account when the investment accounting system is implemented. Examples of data required by the front office, but frequently omitted, include the following:

- Enabling the allocation of cash to discrete 'sub-portfolios' (eg through the creation of a notional 'UK Equity Sub-Portfolio') for segregated multi-market funds managed by more than one market specialist. This is important for asset allocation purposes, in order that there is a mechanism by which cash can be notionally withdrawn from one sub-portfolio and injected into another.

- Linking of dividends (preferably entitlements) to the stocks generating them. This is key to enabling accurate performance analysis

- Data set up to facilitate the link between a unitized vehicle in its guise as an investing fund and as a security held by other funds

Economic research data from Datastream, Bloomberg etc is required to enable analysts to identify how trends in economic fundamentals (eg gross domestic product, interest rates, oil price) affect securities markets.

A very brief summary of the types of data required by each desk is as follows.

Equity Management

- ▶ Security classification (industry – multiple levels, different schemes from different suppliers, market, currency, 'theme', company size)

- ▶ Security specific data (price (including history), earnings, dividend yield, beta)

- ▶ Stock level indices

- ▶ Index Constituent Flag

- ▶ Number of shares in issue

- ▶ Price

- ▶ Indexed security news service

Fixed Interest Management

- ▶ Stock level indices

- ▶ Index constituent flag

- ▶ Prior charge capital/amount outstanding

- ▶ Gross price

Currency Management

- ▶ Spot rates

- ▶ Cross rates

- ▶ Interest rates

Treasury

- ▶ Short-term interest rates

APPENDIX I

Leverage

Leverage is generically where you get more for less. Although this principle applies to a certain extent in the asset management world it is combined with another principle, this being that there is no such thing as a free lunch.

Physical vs Derivatives

Physical

When investing through the physical market (ie normal equities, bonds, property and money market instruments), the fund manager gains an amount of exposure to a particular security by paying for it (virtually) immediately. This payment is an amount of cash equal and opposite to the exposure gained. Therefore if a fund manager decides he wants to increase his exposure to the UK market by £5,650,000, and his analysts are telling him that BSkyB is looking cheap at the current time, then he might instruct his dealers to carry out the following transactions.

Security	Transaction Type	Nominal	Price	Exposure/ Consideration
BSkyB	BUY	1,000,000	565p	£5,650,000
Sterling Cash	PAY	5,650,000	£1	£5,650,000

This increases his exposure to the UK market by £5,650,000, and reduces his exposure to Sterling Cash by the same amount, ie it is costing him £5,650,000 in cash now to increase his exposure to the UK by the same amount.

Derivatives

If allowable in the fund's charter, the fund manager could, alternatively, increase his exposure to the UK by taking out a long futures position in a contract such as the LIFFE FTSE 100 series. If he did this, he would only need to pay out a small amount of cash (this being roughly equivalent to the maximum amount that LIFFE calculate that the position could lose in one day). The transactions involved might be as follows.

Security	Transaction Type	Number of Contracts Nominal	Price	Exposure/ Consideration
LIFFE FTSE 100 Sept	OPEN	9	6,500	£5,850,000
Sterling Cash	PAY	65,000	£1	£65,000

The number of contracts is calculated as:

$$\frac{Exposure\_Required}{Contract\_Size\_x\_Index\_Level}$$

Here the exposure required is £5,850,000, the contract size is 100 (for the LIFFE FTSE contracts) and the index level was 6,500. Note that the exposure actually obtained is higher than that initially required, since the number of contracts has been rounded (it is not possible to open positions using fractions of contracts).

Comparing Physical with Derivatives

We can now see the leverage potential available to the fund manager, by comparing the amount of cash required to gain the required exposure.

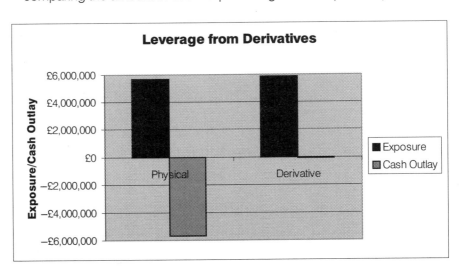

As can be seen, by using derivatives the fund manager only has to pay out a tiny fraction of the cash amount required to gain the exposure through the use of physical securities. The fund manager could, on the basis used above, use the cash required to purchase physical securities to open a position giving him £526,500,000 of exposure to the UK market!

Other Methods Used to Leverage a Portfolio

▶ Borrowing (either intentionally, or by going overdrawn)

▶ Short selling

▶ Buying high beta equities or increasing fixed-interest portfolio duration

APPENDIX II

Covered Interest Arbitrage Rule

In foreign exchange markets, forward rates are determined by interest rate differentials between markets. Thus, if interest rates in one country are higher than those in another, the forward rate will be higher than the spot rate, this being known as the 'forward premium'. Similarly, a forward discount will apply to the forward exchange rate where interest rates in one economy are lower than those in another.

If this rule did not apply, then traders would be able to convert funds into a currency with a higher interest rate than their base currency at a given spot rate, sell the currency forward at the same rate, earn the higher interest rate for the duration of the forward contract and finally convert back at the locked in forward rate. This trade is known as covered interest arbitrage.

Calculating Forward Rates

If we were dealing three month forward for dollar/yen, dealers would consider the current dollar/yen exchange rate, and the differentials in three month euro-currency interest rates for the US dollar and Japanese yen.

If the current spot rate for dollar/yen is 121.7 and three month interest rates for the currencies are 5.4375% and 0.375% respectively, then using the formula:

$$\frac{X_F}{X_O} = \frac{1 + (R_y/4)}{1 + (R_\$/4)}$$

Where:　　X_F is the forward exchange rate

X_O is the current spot rate

R_Y is the three month euroyen interest rate

$R_\$$ is the three month eurodollar interest rate

the forward rate is calculated as:

$$\frac{XF}{121.7} = \frac{1(+ (00375/4)}{1 + (054375/4)} = 120.1084$$

The difference is often quoted as an annualized premium (if interest rates in the first currency are higher) or discount. In this case it would be:

$$\left(\frac{121.7}{120.1084}\right) \times 4 = 4.051\,\text{yen}$$

This forward premium exists because otherwise it would be possible to borrow money in euroyen at 0.375% , convert it to US dollars at the current exchange rate of 121.7, put it on deposit in eurodollars at 5.4375% for three months and convert it back in three months' time at the same rate, thereby making a risk free profit.

Explaining **H**ome Bias in Portfolio Construction

Introduction

'Home bias' is the empirical observation that investors hold too little of their portfolios in foreign assets when compared to the levels predicted by modern portfolio theory. The theory states that portfolios would achieve a better Sharpe (return/risk) ratio[37] through increased diversification by holding higher percentages in foreign assets and would, therefore, enjoy better long-term performance. This improvement is achieved through low correlations of returns across markets (ie when one is performing badly, another is performing well). The fact that portfolios do not diversify internationally as predicted has led to the development of explanatory theories regarding this apparently irrational behaviour.

The Evidence

Lewis (1999) constructed an artificial US-domiciled mutual fund (the home bias puzzle is particularly prevalent in the United States) of portfolios constructed from two asset classes: US equities, represented by the S&P 500[38] index, and foreign equities, represented by the Morgan Stanley EAFE[39] index. Using mean and standard deviation data for monthly returns from January 1970 to December 1996, a simplified efficient frontier is plotted, showing combinations of US and EAFE stocks from 100% US to 100% EAFE.

Lewis' analysis is supported by the following (summarized) statistics.

---

[37] Sharpe ratio calculated as excess return of equity portfolio over risk-free rate (US Treasury Bills) divided by portfolio standard deviation.
[38] Index constructed and maintained by Standard and Poors of the 500 largest US stocks by market capitalization.
[39] Index similarly constructed from large stocks in Europe, Australia and Far East (EAFE).

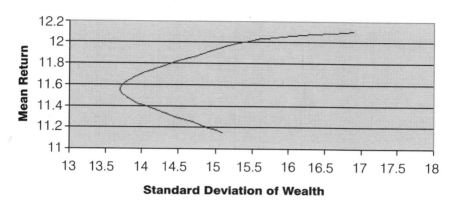

Risk/Return Trade-off for US/EAFE Investment

	Mean Return	Standard Deviation
US	11.14	15.07
EAFE	12.12	16.85

The correlation coefficient calculated between US and EAFE was 0.48 (ie relatively low), thereby creating the opportunity to construct a better risk/ reward optimized portfolio from these two asset classes.

This evidence is supported by a more recent and similar study by Mezrich et al (1999) covering the period from 1970 to 1999; although the extremely strong US market has a superior average return at a lower risk, the Sharpe ratio for the portfolio is still maximized with a 30% allocation to EAFE stocks.

These analyses highlight the puzzle: why do US fund managers hold around 8% of their portfolios in foreign equities[40] when this is clearly 'inferior' in MPT terms, for example, since a 61% US, 39% foreign allocation would have a lower return for a higher risk?

Explanations

This conclusive evidence of the existence of home bias, and the implications for the management of funds (ie that fund managers are not

---

[40] This actually represents an *increase* since 1980.

maximizing long-term returns because of making non-optimal asset allocation decisions) would imply irrational behaviour. However several strong arguments have been put forward to explain this behaviour.

One theoretical justification is that home equities provide a better hedge for home risks. All funds exist to provide fund stakeholders with a capital sum or income stream at a point in the future. These liabilities, all typically payable in the domestic currency, are at risk from the influence of domestic inflation. Since empirical evidence has decisively rejected purchasing power parity (PPP), it is accepted that inflation will vary between countries and was proposed as a reason for home bias. This theory was rejected by a number of studies, however, citing evidence that, *inter alia*, inflation (and exchange rate) risks are priced into international equity returns.

Another theory, that diversification costs exceed the gains, is based on the cost of information and trading costs and taxes not incurred in domestic investment. Information regarding domestic stocks will typically be far more easily available to, and understandable by, domestic fund managers than foreign stock information. One important difference is in accounting standards[41], this being particularly important to fund managers since much of their decision-making analysis is based on earnings data which is itself based on accounts data. Even if it were possible to achieve, the sheer cost in time spent homogenizing such data so that consistent decision making could be carried out across markets could be prohibitive. Trading costs, taxes and other impediments such as capital controls do represent a disincentive to invest in foreign markets especially when compared to more developed domestic markets such as the US, UK and Germany. Empirically, however, these potential explanations do not hold water. From the point of view of information costs, domestic fund managers are just as likely to spurn markets where information is freely available and conforms with familiar standards. Tesar and Werner (1995) found that the turnover of foreign stocks greatly exceeded that of domestic stocks in domestic funds. If trading and other costs were, in fact, a disincentive, one would expect the opposite to be the case.

A third theory put forward is that that home bias is empirically

---

[41] A spectacular example is large Japanese stocks, for which little useful accounts data is available to fund managers.

mismeasured. This has been researched by testing whether mean returns and standard deviations are statistically different between markets, and whether observed portfolio weights and optimal portfolio weights are statistically different from each other. For the US, the hypothesis that there was no difference could not be rejected, although for UK fund managers, the hypothesis was rejected. The implications of the non-rejection of the hypothesis that risk-adjusted returns for US investment were no different from EAFE returns for asset allocation were examined by Pastor (2000). Using the Bayesian approach, ie where no single model captures reality and an investor's behaviour is driven by the level of conviction in his prior beliefs, he applied it to this situation. Pastor concluded that fund managers had a 'strong belief' in the hypothesis that there was no difference between a US-only and a diversified portfolio, resulting in their 8% (sub-optimal) foreign weighting.

His summarized estimated results, with a corresponding standard deviation for strength of belief, were as follows.

Strength of Belief	Standard Deviation	Asset Allocation Weight
Absolutely convinced	0.00	0%
Strong Belief	1.00	8%
Uncertain	3.05	30%

This approach leads, in fact, to a different conclusion; that greater uncertainty regarding the differential between domestic and foreign risk-adjusted returns would result in *higher* foreign asset allocation. It does not, therefore, really help us greatly with the home bias puzzle.

Summary/Concluding Thoughts

Research into reasons for home bias have not really produced a concrete solution to the home bias puzzle. The theories put forward to explain it, such as the better hedging of home liabilities, diversification cost exceeding benefits and over-estimation of home bias do not stand up to empirical research. Although impossible to test, it is possible that the reasons for continued home bias could be as banal as the persistent bull run in the UK and US, combined with living memories of horror stories relating to foreign investment such as Japan, Russia and Asia Pacific.

APPENDIX IV

Convexity

The relationship defined by modified duration, or volatility, which predicts the change in a bond's price for a given change in yields, only holds for small changes in yields due to the concept of convexity. The convexity of a bond defines the non-linear relationship between bond prices and yields.

Price

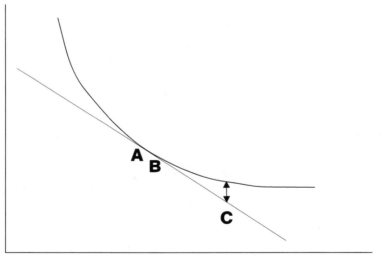

Yield to Maturity

Where yields move a small distance, eg corresponding to the movement from A to B, the difference in the linear estimation of the change in the bond's price can be seen to be pretty much the same as that generated by the non-linear convexity relationship. However, for a large change in yields (eg from A to C), the difference is far greater, making convexity an important consideration.

Convexity is actually a desirable attribute of a bond, or bond portfolio, since if convexity is greater, bond prices/fund values fall relatively less for a given rise in yield. At the same time, a fall in yields will give a greater rise in price/value. In fact, the optimal convexity of a portfolio, which can be increased through buying bonds with higher prices, lower coupons and with call options, would be as follows.

Price

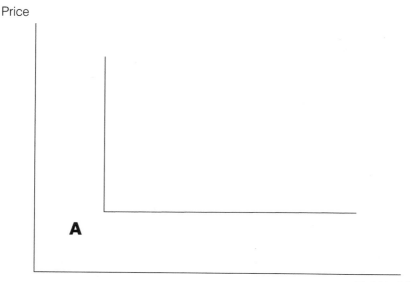

Yield to Maturity

If yields rise from those corresponding to point A, there is no change in the bond's price. However, if yields fall, the price rockets.

The Euro Project

Introduction

The integration of participating European countries' currencies into one single currency is one of the largest projects ever undertaken in the financial world. The main motivation for European Monetary Union (EMU) in general and the euro as the single currency in particular is, however, political rather than economic. It is important to remember that, further to two world wars in the last century, there is an extremely strong desire to prevent further outbreaks of war in europe. Continental europeans believe that the bringing together of nations is the best method of achieving this and have striven to integrate europe in the last 50 years. Thus the euro is only one part of an overall political integration project which includes the european Union's parliament and legal framework, as well as the economic machinery of the european Central Bank (ECB) and agreements on trade in place amongst participating european nations.

Although the prime motivation is to progress european political integration through a common currency, there are potential economic benefits of a successful and strong euro. The main benefit to all participants in this project would be the replacement of the US dollar with the euro as the world's reference currency. The role that the dollar has played since the breakdown of the Bretton Woods fixed exchange rate agreement in the early 1970s has enabled the US to persistently consume far more than it produces (ie run a huge Federal budget deficit). This has been because of the global demand for US dollars which has maintained the currency at a very high level, resulting in relatively high living standards in the US. A similar demand for euro would potentially offer the same benefits to euro-in countries. For many less wealthy european countries there are significant benefits to be gained from participation. These include the lower cost of servicing government debt due to a large reduction in currency risk to lenders.

The costs of this integration project to wealthier countries such as Germany are high. As well as seeing their domestic currency severely depreciate in value against the US dollar, with the long term standard of living reduction that this brings, cost of debt denominated in euro is higher. In addition their governments have lost many of the tools used to fine-tune their economies to the ECB. It is important to remember the broader political agenda when analysing the motivation of wealthier nations.

Brief History

As mentioned, EMU and the euro should be seen as a key milestone in a 50 year process of political and economic integration in europe. The main events are as follows.

Year/Period	Event	Significance
1957	Treaties of Rome signed	Established the foundation for the European Union, initially with core European nations
Early 70s	Bretton Woods Exchange Rate system collapses	European currencies no longer 'pegged' to US dollar. Potential for exchange rate volatility
Early 70s	Formation of European Currency 'Snake'	'Floating peg' system aimed at reducing volatility by preventing participant European currencies from moving outside a given range of each other
Mid 1980s	Exchange Rate Mechanism (ERM) replaces 'snake'	Similar concept to 'snake'

Year/Period	Event	Significance
1992	UK forced out of ERM by currency speculators	Inherent weakness of artificial exchange rate systems exposed. Added momentum to single currency initiative
1 January 1999	Euro launched with 11 initial participants	ECB now responsible for monetary policy on behalf of participants

The key event that has not taken place is UK participation. In order for the euro to be in a position to replace the US dollar as the world's reference currency, it needs an equivalent Gross Domestic Product (GDP) backing. Participation of the UK and other current EMU-out nations would raise euro GDP to around $8 trillion, compared to US GDP of $7.8 trillion.

The current state of play is that the euro is struggling. At the end of the year 2000, it had lost nearly a third of its value against the US dollar, and over 15% against sterling since inception. Despite this, the ECB is generally establishing a credible reputation for sound management.

The Difficulties of Maintaining A Single Currency

The key challenge for the ECB is to define a monetary policy strategy that will promote prosperity in all its participant nations. This is extremely difficult, because EMU countries are influenced by different forces. Spain is likely to be influenced by economic changes in Latin America, due to trading links, whereas Finland's prosperity is influenced by conditions in Russia. Countries may also be at different stages of the economic cycle: while tight monetary policy may be required to underpin low inflation, countries going through a growth phase, such as Ireland and Spain, could find that they lose momentum through a shortage of liquidity.

Additionally the ECB needs to monitor the fiscal policies of EMU participant national governments, in accordance with the Stability and Growth Pact (SGP). This is designed to ensure that participant nations adopt responsible (ie non-expansionary) fiscal policies, thereby protecting the ECB's hard-earned low inflation reputation.

The pressures on the ECB from participant nations has been intense. Less than three months after launch the requirement to maintain interest rates at a given level to maintain the euro's value relative to other currencies led to a stand-off with Germany. The German Finance Minister, Oskar Lafontaine, requested a reduction in euro interest rates to alleviate German domestic unemployment and reduce the risk of a deflationary spiral. When this was refused by ECB chairman Wim Duisenberg, Germany threatened to increase government spending (to alleviate the stated domestic problems). Duisenberg publicly reminded the Germans of their commitment to the SGP, leading to the resignation of Lafontaine. Despite this impressively robust display by the ECB in the face of intense pressure from their largest participant country, market observers questioned the feasibility of a 'one size fits all' monetary policy.

Summary

The euro project is navigating uncharted waters. Never before have a group of developed nations been subject to centrally defined, and occasionally inappropriate, monetary policies. Despite the efforts of the ECB and the cooperation of participant nations, the euro has been very weak relative to the US dollar. This is a clear message from the market that they are not considering the euro as a viable alternative reference currency. The non-participation of the UK is a serious handicap to the euro. Yet it is unlikely that the UK will join with the euro on its knees, creating the possibility of an on-going Catch-22 situation.

Asian Financial Crisis

Introduction

The Asian financial crisis in 1997 has had a severe, detrimental effect on the global financial system, not least in the economies at the heart of the meltdown. This has led to a fundamental and sustained loss of confidence in the region by global investors. In turn this has caused international authorities, including G7 (Group of Seven leading industrial countries), to review the structure of the international monetary system, particularly with regard to emerging and developing markets.

The crisis itself had its epicentre in the ASEAN (Association of South-East Asian Nations) member countries, particularly Thailand, the Philippines, Malaysia and Indonesia, with other economies also being hit, including South Korea. The elements of the crisis were heavy selling of national currencies, resistance to devaluation by central banks, abandonment of pegged exchange rates and capital flight. Fallout from the crisis has also impacted Japan, particularly in the banking sector, where loan books were heavily exposed to developing Asian nations.

This appendix examines the many causes of the crisis including economic factors, the exchange rate systems in place, the role of financial 'speculators', contagion effects and the role of national governments, whose handling of the crisis has been called into question, particularly given the clear precedent in the form of the Mexican financial crisis of 1994. Finally the alternatives for the restructuring of the international monetary system are examined.

Causes

It has been argued that the crisis was inevitable, given the stage of evolution of the economies involved. Given the structure that was in place in the economies at the centre of the maelstrom, perhaps the crisis was inevitable. One could, therefore, also argue that the structure could have been changed. However, as we will see, this would have required a major cultural change on behalf of the governments involved. The reality is that this change is now essential if Asia is to have any chance of attracting investors back to the region.

(a) Economic Factors

This section is divided into two parts since some of the economic parameters involved would generically tend to result in a currency crisis, whereas others were peculiar to the Asian economic community. A significant contributor to the Asian crisis was that the respective governments ignored clear signals that their currencies were overvalued, instead clinging to the 'pegged' exchange rate systems that had worked so well for them in the past.

(i) Economic Fundamentals

One of the main catalysts of the initial stages of the crisis in Thailand, and of the overall crisis, was a marked decline in the growth of exports, principally in the electronics market. There were no sinister causes of this; it was simply a cyclical reduction in demand for Personal Computers, after several years of spectacular growth, causing knock-on reductions in demand for the components manufactured cheaply in Asia. The impact on Asian countries in general, and Thailand in particular, was very severe, however. In Thailand it caused a further deterioration in the current account deficit. In addition, it affected the budget balance, creating a fiscal deficit after a decade of strong and stable fiscal surpluses. These developments, in conjunction with the heavy reliance on foreign investment (although the savings rate was high, internally generated funds were not sufficient to finance investment needs), meant that Thailand had a huge external funding requirement, the biggest in Asia.

These factors, the enormous current account deficit, a worrying fiscal situation, over-dependence on foreign capital and increasing debt resulted in a downgrading of Thailand by Moody's credit rating agency. However, because of the pegged exchange rate system the US dollar–Thai baht rate remained virtually unchanged. This, incidentally, caused further problems since the US dollar – Japanese yen exchange rate had risen steadily through 1995 and 1996, making Thai goods less competitive.

(ii) Asia-Specific Factors

Given this clear misalignment between economic fundamentals and the exchange rate, why did the ASEAN economies not simply allow their currencies to devalue? The reluctance to devalue was largely due to the perceived loss of prestige that the political leaders of these economies felt they would suffer. After many years of espousing the virtues of Asian industriousness, devaluation was seen as an admission of failure, rather than a natural adjustment given a cyclical downturn.

Another contributing factor is generally described as 'crony capitalism': each government's (too) close involvement and interference in the running of the economy helped to create asset price bubbles, particularly in the property market, the bursting of which was the basis of the crisis. This was due to what is described as 'moral hazard', where investors were under the (false) impression that their investments were effectively underwritten by the government. In general, investors had incomplete information regarding the nature of the risks of their investment, this being an unhealthy result of the cosy relationship between the banks and the government (not to mention the virtual absence of regulations like capital adequacy). This meant that capital flowed into riskier, overpriced investments (investors perceiving that they effectively had a 'put' option – either the investment would succeed giving high returns, or the government would give them their money back). Research has shown that it was these asset price bubbles that caused the flight of capital and contributed to the collapse of currencies, rather than fiscal deficits (cause of 'first generation' currency crises) or the temptation of governments to abandon the pegged system to expand the economy ('second generation' currency crisis model). Some analysts also demonstrated the existence of ASEAN-specific price bubbles through the comparison of aggregate stock prices against dividends. While ASEAN countries showed a departure from a normal relationship between equity prices and dividends, Australia and Japan continued the normal relationship, despite the fact that Japan was heavily embroiled in the crisis for a time.

The political structure of many countries at the heart of the crisis added momentum to the flight of capital once the crisis had got under way. International investors turned a blind eye to the scandals, corruption and civil unrest in many countries, since the returns offered on investment were too good to miss. However, the levels of confidence in regimes often reliant on autocratic and/or inexperienced governments plummeted as the depth of the crisis, and the underlying weaknesses of the economies involved, became clear.

Over-reliance on foreign investment with the (realized) risk that funds can quickly be withdrawn, was another factor which fanned the flames of the crisis. Although the financing of Asian investment had evolved from direct investment through bank loans to equity financing, thereby bringing into the market foreign pension fund investment, this actually made it easier for capital to leave the country (fund managers simply sell their shares, whereas it is more difficult for bankers to recover loans).

Government handling of the crisis clearly made the situation worse than it might otherwise have been. In particular the hysterical behaviour of the Malaysian Prime Minister, and the introduction of capital controls has, and is continuing to, drive away many institutional investors, probably for the foreseeable future. The 'come-what-may' defending of exchange rates clearly out of line with economic fundamentals exacerbated the crisis by burning up invaluable foreign currency reserves much needed to cover imports. An element of naivety was demonstrated here, ASEAN governments believing that they could, in the words of Margaret Thatcher, 'buck the markets', when the Bank of England with its vast reserves had failed to defend sterling against currency speculators in 1992. In addition the tactic adopted by many central banks of hiking short-term interest rates to deter speculators was not effective in defending the currency, although some speculators were initially hurt. A side effect was that short-term interest rates of up to 1,500% annualized had a further detrimental effect on domestic companies.

(a)   Pegged Exchange Rate Structure

All of the economies deeply affected by the crisis were operating a pegged exchange rate structure. The original objective of this was to create a stable environment for investors, where they would be confident that the value of their investments would not be decayed by currency devaluation.

However, fixed exchange rate regimes like this can only work, given the presence of international currency speculators, if the exchange rate is in line with economic fundamentals so that Purchasing Power Parity (ie, where similar goods cost the same in common currency terms in different countries) prevails. Latterly, this point seems to have escaped the ASEAN central banks, who spent fortunes defending their currencies at unsustainable exchange rates, when all of the standard measures (debt service ratio, import ratio, variance of export revenue and domestic money supply growth) were clearly indicating that a correction was required.

It is perhaps understandable that the Asian governments persisted with this policy, given its success in the past. To be fair, most of the economies involved were probably at a crossroads where floating exchange rates had become more appropriate. However, the use of floating exchange rates, with all the benefits of easy adjustment (Friedman (1953) argued that other economic variables are much more difficult to adjust than exchange rates), was not acceptable to Asian politicians at that time. The empirical evidence strongly supports the assertion that currencies cannot be defended against speculators where there are strong reasons why a currency should be devalued. Although it may be possible to smooth a change in exchange rates to give the underlying economy a chance to adjust, pouring millions of dollars into the FX markets simply gives the speculators a counterparty to trade with.

(c)   *Contagion*

There are clear indications that the demise of the Thai baht encouraged speculators to attack other currencies, where the corresponding economies had similar profiles. Contagion can be ruled out as a significant causal factor since the effects of the crisis, particularly in the longer term, have been far more muted systems in more established economies in the region (eg Singapore), with floating exchange rates.

(d)   *Role of Speculators*

Contrary to the rantings of the Malaysian Prime Minister, the 'speculators' clearly did not cause the crisis. They were merely fulfilling their role in the financial system, as arbitrageurs between the current, fixed exchange rate level and the level that the currency should have been trading at, given economic fundamentals. There is no evidence to suggest self-fulfilling attacks on the Asian currencies; all empirical research points to anticipation of a devaluation, justified through identification of asset price bubbles.

Implications for Future Restructuring of International Monetary System

The Asian financial crisis shook the global financial system to its foundations; many investors lost huge amounts on defaulting debts and sharp falls in equity values, as well as on the currencies themselves. This, combined with the hardship caused throughout Asia, has led to a fresh review of the system, particularly in terms of global regulation. The main objective of this review is to provide an environment in which, to paraphrase Alan Greenspan, sustainable, non-inflationary, productivity-oriented growth can occur.

Many new 'blueprints' have been put forward for restructuring. The following is a review of the areas considered by would-be policymakers, along with their respective pros and cons. The blueprints tend to be combinations of these policies. The task of defining a blueprint is a difficult one, however. The main objectives of continuing national sovereignty, regulated and cushioned markets and the benefits of global capital markets are, according to Larry Summers, US Deputy Treasury Secretary, 'an impossible trinity'. The task is certainly extremely complex, having to balance the benefits and costs of fixed and floating exchange rate systems, capital controls and capital adequacy requirements, whilst requiring commitment to greater disclosure. Add to this different cultures and the moral hazard problem encountered in many emerging markets and one can see the enormity of the task.

The respective roles of the International Monetary Fund (IMF), the Bank for International Settlements (BIS) and the World Bank have yet to be clearly established. However, they have committed to participate in a new 'financial stability forum', proposals for which have been put forward by Hans Tietmeyer of the German Bundesbank, these having been endorsed at the February 2000 G7 meeting.

(a) Exchange Rate System
A world of floating exchange rates has many attractions, including the

retention of domestic monetary policy in the hands of national governments, the forcing of firms and investors to hedge their currency risk and empirically less severe (although more frequent) currency crises. The main drawback for the economies at the heart of the Asian crisis is the volatility that tends to be caused by large capital inflows and outflows, due in part to the relatively small size of these economies to investors such as pension funds. These flows can cause huge volatility in exchange rates, which tends to deter investors. The establishment of fixed exchange rates seeks to reduce this volatility through pegging the national currency to a stronger currency, usually the US dollar. This is not sufficient on its own, however: this exchange rate must reflect the true underlying value of the currency (based on PPP measures). Only then can governments successfully defend currencies against speculators through intervention. If and when the exchange rate set moves out of line with underlying fundamentals the government must change the rate, and possibly intervene to smooth the passage of the currency to the new rate.

(b) Capital Controls

As stated above, the relatively huge flows of capital can create volatility in markets. This can lead to panic selling as well as uncertainty regarding funding of investment projects (in the long run leading to fewer projects with a worse risk/return profile). To avoid this problem, the introduction of capital controls has been put forward, limiting the rate and size of capital flows. The main problem with this approach is that it is not really acceptable to global investors, who require capital mobility. Better perhaps would be to balance the economy's funding portfolio through the attraction of more longer-term investors such as pension and mutual fund managers.

(c) Disclosure

The lack of accurate and perhaps truthful information regarding investment in South-East Asia clearly contributed to the growth of asset price bubbles in the region. For international supervision of financial markets to work, effective surveillance is required to provide early indicators of impending crises (eg if currencies/assets are becoming overvalued). The series of measures put forward by Hans Tietmeyer attempted to introduce reporting standards and monetary and financial transparency. It remains to be seen to what degree countries will comply with these requirements.

(d) Capital Adequacy

The capital adequacy requirements set out in the Basle Accord of 1988 provide a structure for controlling global capital allocation at source. The requirement is that lenders retain a proportion of *risk-weighted* assets in short-dated investments or cash (thereby reducing returns). This mechanism could be used to allocate a higher risk factor to investments in countries which either have weak fundamentals or poor reporting standards or both. This would both prevent asset price bubbles from forming, and encourage better disclosure.

(e) Managing the Speculators

Through sound economic management, the formation of asset price bubbles and overvalued currencies can be avoided. This will reduce speculative attacks significantly. Given this, the defence of a currency against an unjustified attack is more likely to succeed, particularly if supported by the international financial community.

Summary

It is clear that market prices, (eg exchange rates, bond yields and equity prices) need to transparently reflect the underlying value of an investment in any economy, also taking into account the risks involved, including the track record of its national regulators. What is less clear is how countries can be incentivized to follow prudent practice on the one hand, and how investors can be provided with more accurate data to make better risk-adjusted investment decisions on the other.

It is also clear that no artificial mechanism, eg fixed exchange rates or capital controls, is a substitute for sound and realistic economic and financial management. Adherence to reporting standards and requirements by all countries is essential if the international financial community is to be able to manage the international monetary system.

Fund managers were badly burned by the Asian financial crisis. Asset allocation to the Asia Pacific region generally remains at a very low level, whilst in Malaysia (which introduced capital controls making it illegal to withdraw funds) investment by equity fund managers is virtually zero. In fact, the FT Actuaries World Equity index – widely used as a benchmark for global equity investment – has a zero allocation to Malaysia. This situation is likely to continue until reporting standards for Asian equities begin to rise to the standards found in more established markets, such as the US and the UK, in terms of accuracy, transparency and credibility. Wider macroeconomic issues such as currency management also need attention. The difficult balance of sound economic management, stable exchange rates and a willingness to allow exchange rates to float freely must be achieved if institutional investors are to be enticed back to the market to provide their previous levels of equity funding.

Bond Market Risk Case Study: Russian Default on Soviet Era Debt

Background

During 1991 and 1992 it became increasingly clear that the newly formed democratic governments which replaced the Union of Soviet Socialist Republics (USSR) were not going to be able to bear the burden of outstanding debt to Western nations such as Germany and the United States. The ensuing negotiations between Western bankers and representatives from the new governments resulted in what has been one of the most complex debt rescheduling exercises in financial history.

For many years up to and including 1991, the former Soviet Union borrowed huge amounts of capital from Western nations. The communist administration used the capital to keep its economy going, resulting in the effective loss of economic sovereignty. The debt was serviced through the delivery of 'hard' currency (ie US dollars or deutschmarks) obtained through exports of the USSR's three most valuable natural resources, oil, gold and precious stones.

After the demise of the communist regime, the new government faced falling oil production and foreign sales as it grappled with the task of replacing the old Soviet economic machinery with a capitalist style structure. This immediately severely reduced the new administrator's ability to meet interest payments, which were all to be paid in hard currency.

The situation was extremely serious; aside from the risk of total bankruptcy of the former USSR itself the dramatic fall in the quality of banks' loan portfolios resulted in the virtual 'crowding out' of other low quality government debtors as banks desperately sought to balance the risks in their loan portfolios. In addition, commodity prices, such as grain, fell since the former USSR could no longer afford to purchase surplus US production. For this reason and others it was clearly in the West's interests to support the rescheduling of Soviet era debt repayments.

Issues

One of the fundamental precepts of this situation is that neither the new former Soviet governments, nor the Western banks that had loaned the capital could afford a total default on the debt to occur. For the former Soviet governments a total default would have resulted in their virtually immediate relegation to the ranks of third world countries unable to access commercial sector financing. Instead they would be totally reliant on global institutions such as the World Bank and the International Monetary Fund, who impose severe economic targets and restrictions on borrowing countries. For the Western banks, including Deutsche Bank, their exposure to the former USSR was extreme. The total writing off of the debt would have been very painful indeed. The resulting situation was extremely finely balanced; whilst wanting to recover as much capital and interest as possible, the banks needed to ensure that they did not bankrupt the former Soviet governments, which would result in total default. An additional concern of Western governments was the servicing of this debt through the sale of arms to undesirable nations.

The issues surrounding this default are complex, thereby making the task of recovering capital all the more difficult. The new political structure of countries constituting the former Soviet Union is, post-glasnost, significantly different. The entity that the loans were made to has, essentially, ceased to exist. In its place, a large number of smaller republics and other political entities came into being. Putting aside any political considerations, from a purely logical point of view the fragmentation of the Soviet Union posed significant problems; how could one apportion the debt across countries (by population?, proportion of loan allocated to each region?, income generation capacity? etc). Similarly the apportionment of former Soviet assets being held by the (former) Soviet State Bank, Gosbank (eg gold, oil and international assets) was far from straightforward.

Further, it became clear that the financial apparatus of the old Soviet Union was inadequate to cope with the requirements of the new order in a 'normal' situation, let alone this crisis situation. The reform of the financial system was particularly difficult due to each government's desire for control over its own affairs. The formation of a 'central bank' to control the interests of all governments within the former Soviet Union was clearly required, but difficult to implement.

As the situation developed, the Russian government took a strong lead in the negotiations with Western banks, in the management of former Soviet assets and in the coordination of former Soviet governments (not easy since some were actually at war with each other). Without this lead, and the 'single point of contact' that the Russian government under Boris Yeltsin represented it is hard to see how the situation would have been easily resolved.

One of the main problems faced by the former Soviet governments was liquidity, particularly in hard currency terms. An early concession by the Western banks, referred to collectively as the 'Paris Club' was the rescheduling of short maturity payments (in this case due in the following two years) to further out.

Summary

The lessons to investors from the Soviet era debt crisis are numerous. Many major league investors were lured into the Soviet Union by the very high yields being offered by the then current government. 'Political risk' was generally treated as a largely theoretical threat. This episode also clearly demonstrates the benefits of portfolio diversification, ie spreading your risk across a number of uncorrelated asset classes. Risk and reward are clearly demonstrated; despite the attractive yields on offer from this type of loan we can clearly see the quid pro quo, namely a gigantic fall in the value of this debt, and uncertainty as to receipt of future cash flows.

Overview of Modern Forecasting Techniques

Background

Like most financial institutions, asset managers are required to forecast future returns from different markets before allocating their clients' funds so as to provide a superior return on their clients' investment. This task has become increasingly difficult over recent years as markets seem to behave independently of traditional 'value' measures such as P/E ratios. At the same time, techniques continue to advance in the field of financial forecasting, both in the enhancement of econometric models and in the development of Artificial Neural Networks (ANNs) technology, particularly with respect to time series analysis. The purpose of this appendix is to give an overview of some of these new tools.

Introduction

As discussed in the introduction, the role of asset managers is to maximize returns to their clients by investing the clients' funds in those assets offering superior returns. Assets are generally grouped into discrete markets, eg UK equities, US bonds etc, for the purpose of allocating assets on a 'top down' basis, eg allocating a given percentage to UK equities, and then allocating funds from this percentage to certain preferred stocks within UK equities. This allocation process is carried out within a carefully specified framework, designed to control the long-term risk to the fund, and encompassing specific market constraints in addition to minimum investor return requirements. This framework is the fund's 'benchmark' and is defined by the trustees of the fund, along with the maximum permitted deviations from the benchmark (generally known as the fund's 'constraints'). The main inputs to this asset allocation process are forecast returns from now to an investment horizon defined for the purpose of making choices between market segments. These horizons vary between asset management houses, but are generally of the order of one to three months. This is particularly the case within equity markets where it is less easy to move in and out of large positions than in more liquid markets such as fixed interest and money markets (where horizons for strategies might be of the order of a couple of weeks). Also required is data showing the relative riskiness of combinations of allocations. As outlined in Chapter 3, portfolio theory suggests that these inputs should be used to construct an 'optimal portfolio', being the combination of assets offering the highest overall return for the lowest risk. Although the risk of a particular asset class can be fairly well estimated at any given point in time, the forecasting of returns has proved exceptionally difficult in recent years.

Developments in forecasting techniques in recent years have focused on dependence of future values in a time-series upon values in previous periods and on 'patterns' present in the time-series. Econometric models have been developed to take account of empirically observed features of economic time series data. These new models deviate from the assumptions underlying the Classical Linear Regression Model (CLRM), and include non-linearity of functional form, non-constant variable mean and non-constant variance of error terms.

In response to poor results from forecasting using traditional methods, new types of econometric models, such as those allowing future values to be conditional upon the values and error terms in previous periods, have been developed. In addition to these econometric models, ANNs for time series forecasting of financial markets are also tested. These systems differ from econometric models in that there is no requirement to specify a model. Rather, they identify patterns in data through being supplied with a number of (relevant) inputs and the actual output[42] and through a process of 'learning' they identify patterns in the data which enable them to forecast the next value in the series.

In the interests of maintaining the flow of ideas, econometric models are separated from Artificial Neural Networks in the following summary.

---

[42] Strictly speaking, this only applies to one type of ANN architecture, the supervised network.

It should be clearly borne in mind that the objective of this Appendix is purely to stimulate interest in modern techniques; further reading and study is recommended if this objective is met.

Overview of New Techniques
I   Econometric Models

(a) Background Theory

The new generation of econometric models aim to define parametric models which predict a dependent variable (such as the next value of the FTSE All Share index) from a set of independent variables, whilst coping with departures from the assumptions underlying the Classical Linear Regression Model (CLRM). The CLRM is based upon 10 assumptions, summarized as follows (Gujerati, 1995):

(1) The regression model is linear in the parameters, ie specified in the form

$$Y_1 = \beta_1 + \beta_2 X_i + u_1$$

where: Y_i is the dependent variable

           X_i is the independent variable

           β_1 is the intercept

           β_2 is the coefficient of independent variable X

           u_i is the error term

(2)   Independent (X) values are fixed in repeated sampling

(3)   Zero mean value of disturbance u_i

(4)   Homoscedasticity or equal variance of u_i

(5)   No autocorrelation between the disturbances in the time series

(6)   Zero covariance between u_i and X_i

(7)   The number of observations n must be greater than the number of parameters to be estimated

(8)   Variability in X values (ie they must not all be the same)

(9) The regression model is correctly specified, ie there is no specification bias

(10) There is no perfect multicolinearity (ie there are no perfect linear relationships among the explanatory variables)

It has become abundantly evident that the imposition of these restrictions on the model renders the CLRM useless for predicting next values of economic time series. It is in response to this failure that modern econometric tools have been developed.

(b) The Modern Econometrician's Toolkit
Econometricians now have what could be viewed as a 'toolkit' with which to define forecasting models, along with a number of tests designed to measure the significance of results obtained. The newer 'tools' are designed to cope with departures from the assumptions specified above, and are variously combined to produce specific models. The constituent tools can be specified as follows.

Autoregressive (AR) Process
Where a value Y at time period $t+1$ (Y_{t+1}) depends on the value of Y_t, it is said to follow a first order autoregressive or AR(1) process. Thus the model would be specified in the form:

$$Y_t = \alpha_1(Y_{t-1}) + \alpha_2(Y_{t-2}) + \ldots \alpha_p (Y_{t-p}) + u_t$$

where: Y_t is the dependent variable's value at time period t (ie the one we wish to predict)

Y_p is the pth lagged value of the independent variable, ie the value p periods ago

a_p is the coefficient of the lagged value of the independent variable at period p

u_i is the error term

ie one (or more) of the explanatory variables for Y is one (or more) of its own lagged values. Where more than one lagged value is used (eg n lagged values) the autoregressive process is denoted as AR(n).

Moving Average (MA) Scheme

The Moving Average (MA) tool is used to cope with the presence of autocorrelation. Autocorrelation in the context of time-series regression refers to a pattern existing amongst the error terms in a time-series. This is a departure from Assumption (5) of the CLRM. Any number of adjacent error terms in the time-series can be included in the moving average; an MA(p) scheme can be defined as:

$$Y_1 = \beta_1 u_{t-1} + \beta_1 u_{t-2} + \dots \beta_p u_{t-p} + u_1$$

where: Y_t is the dependent variable's value at time period t (ie the one we wish to predict)

u_{t-p} is the lagged value of the error term in period t–p, ie the error term p periods ago

b_p is the coefficient of the lagged value of the independent variable at period p

u_i is the error term for the current time period

ie in this case Y is a linear combination of the current and p lagged error terms.

Integrated (I) Series

It has been found that many financial time-series do not have a constant mean and variance through time. If one examines time-series data for stock market indices, one can quickly see that, for discrete time periods of the same duration but at different points in time, the moments (ie the mean, variance and covariances with other variables of interest) are different. Where this variation in the moments through time exists, the series is said to be non-stationary. In order that analysis of a time-series can provide meaningful results, it must be stable, or stationary. Non-stationary series are, therefore, differenced in order to produce a stationary series, this differencing being carried out any number of times until a stationary series is produced[43]. Differencing is simply a case of subtracting the previous value from each value in the time-series, ie:

$$X_t - X_{t-1}$$

---

[43] In practice it is rare that more than two differences are required to produce a stationary series.

The number of differences required to produce a stationary time-series indicates the order of integration of the series. Thus if two differences are required, the series is said to be integrated of order two, or I(2).

Autoregressive Conditional Heteroscedastic (ARCH) Process (Engle 1982)

Relaxing Assumption (4) of the CLRM, ie that the variance of the error term is constant through time, is essential for real-life forecasting. Empirical study has revealed clusters of high variances, centring on events such as the 1973 Oil Crisis and Black Monday in 1987. The purpose of an ARCH process is to make the variance of the error term in time $t+1$ conditional upon the variance of the error term in previous periods. Thus a process whereby the variance in time $t+1$ is dependent upon the variance in two lagged periods is specified as an ARCH(2) process. An example of this approach is an ARCH(4) model, where the variance of the error for time period 0 (h_t) is a function of a stochastic variable representing the observed error variance for the current period (0) and the error terms for previous periods. The error term variances for previous periods are weighted to give greater import to more recent terms:

$$h_t = \alpha_0 + \alpha_1 (0.4\ \varepsilon^2_{t-1} + 0.3\ \varepsilon^2_{t-2} + 0.2\ \varepsilon^2_{t-3} + 0.1\ \varepsilon^2_{t-4})$$

Generalized Autoregressive Conditional Heteroscedastic (GARCH) Process

Engle's (1982) initial work was extended by Bollerslev (1986) to allow the heteroscedastic variance of the model to include moving average as well as autoregressive components. The chief benefit of this tool is that a high order ARCH model (ie one that is dependent upon a large number of lagged error terms) may have a more parsimonious GARCH representation.

Vector Autoregression (VAR)

Empirical research has shown the existence of 'feedback' between (so-called) independent variables and the dependent variable, ie that the time-series of the independent variable is affected by changes in the dependent variable. VAR analysis seeks to treat all variables symmetrically, thereby avoiding the issues of dependence and independence.

Exponential GARCH (EGARCH)

A further feature of time-series data is that responses to conditional variance are asymmetric; for example volatility in stock markets is higher after a sharp downturn than a sharp upswing (otherwise known as panic). The EGARCH model allows for this asymmetric response.

(b) Artificial Neural Networks

Artificial Neural Networks (ANNs) are computer software systems which mimic the processes carried out by biological systems, particularly the human brain. In particular, it is the pattern classification and recognition capabilities of the brain that ANNs seek to replicate, by learning and generalizing from experience. ANNs are being developed to serve a broad range of industrial and scientific applications (Widrow et al, 1994), with a major application area being forecasting (Sharda, 1994).

ANNs are, potentially, particularly well suited to the role of forecasting. One of the main advantages over traditional methods is that they are not model based. This removes some of the main problems concerning traditional methods, which is the correct specification of the model, particularly where the relationship is non-linear. Instead of this ANNs 'learn' from examples, capturing subtle functional relationships between variables, where these relationships may be difficult to specify in a model (Zhang et al, 1997). It is important, therefore, that a substantial quantity of data is available in order to initially 'teach' and subsequently test the ANN. The key ability of ANNs is generalization. Having been presented with a sample of data, ANNs can often infer the unseen part of a population, this being analogous to 'learning from experience'.

How do ANNs Work?

The following high level description is based upon 'feedforward' multi-layer perceptron (MLP) type ANNs. As discussed briefly in the next section, there are different types of ANNs, but the general concept and purpose of them is the same.

ANNs are self-adaptive systems, adjusting themselves on the basis of new data being presented to them, thereby improving their predictive power. The adjustment takes place through the changing of weights which, crudely speaking, reflect the relative importance of the independent variables being presented in the data set to the dependent variable.

ANNs are constructed from a number of elements known as neurons or nodes, each of which carries out a simple processing task by taking an input, processing it and producing an output. These nodes are organized into interconnected layers, starting with data external to the ANN, continuing with processing or 'hidden' layers and finishing with an output (ie the dependent variable).

The node connectors are known as 'arcs', which 'feedforward' data from a lower layer to a higher layer. These arcs are intelligent in that they have weights assigned to them, which determine what is fed forward to the next layer. The determination of these weights forms a key part of the training of the ANN, which is carried out before the ANN is used to perform forecasting tasks.

The role of the hidden layers is to provide interim processing of data, typically to classify data by finding a separating line between discrete patterns in the data. The relationship between the inputs and outputs between nodes is determined by the 'activation' (or 'transfer') function,

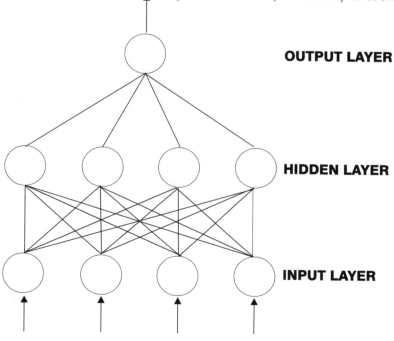

OUTPUT LAYER

HIDDEN LAYER

INPUT LAYER

which essentially determines what data is fed forward to which nodes in the next layer. This function can be determined by the designer of the ANN and importantly can be non-linear, the most popular being the sigmoid or logistic function.

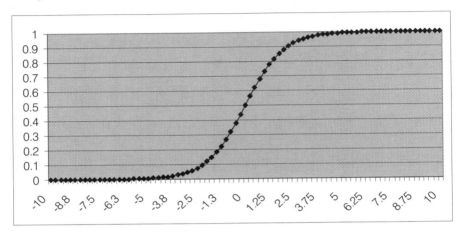

The type of inputs used will depend upon the type of problem being tackled: for causal forecasting problems inputs will be the independent or predictor variables, whereas for time-series forecasting problems the inputs are the past observations. One key advantage of ANNs is that one can easily combine both of these types of data in the same ANN model.

The training of an ANN is carried out by presenting it with a series of inputs (in the form of vectors of input variables) along with a corresponding target output. Using a feedback mechanism known as the error back-propagation algorithm, the ANN will adjust the arc weights connecting the nodes in order to enable it to compute the output from the input. At the conclusion of the training programme, the ANN finds the set of arc weights that minimize the errors (ie the deviation of results calculated by the ANN models from the target results provided in the data set).

Development of ANN Theory: Types of ANNs
Two categories of ANNs have been proposed:

> ▶ 'Feedforward', where outputs from a set of units are connected only to the inputs of the units in the next layer

> ▶ 'Recurrent', where connections are allowed between units in both directions

Interest in recurrent networks, such as Hopfield networks, has declined since the mid-1980s. The reasons for this were the relatively poor pattern storage capacity of this network type. In addition, the attractive feedback feature provided by bi-directional connectivity has been replicated in feedforward ANNs with the development of the error back-propagation algorithm for the training of multi-layer perceptrons.

The most popular type of feedforward ANNs are MLPs described briefly above; however, two other models have gained prominence, Kohonen's self-organizing network and Radial Basis Function networks.

Kohonen's work was inspired by the way in which the brain spatially orders neurons in its sensory pathways in response to the stimulus being sensed. The main difference between this type of network and MLPs is that the neurons are organized in a 'feature map' where their position on this map is determined by the training data sets presented to it, rather than the weighted arc approach of the MLP.

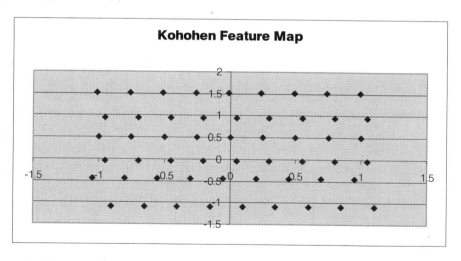

Kohohen Feature Map

As the network is trained, a given input pattern will activate only those neurons corresponding with the position of the input pattern on the map.

Radial Basis Function (RBF) networks play a very similar role to MLPs in that they both provide techniques for approximating arbitrary non-linear functional mappings between an input vector x and a set of outputs y (Bishop, 1995). The key difference lies in the activation function: the MLP transforms inputs using a common activation function, whereas the RBF seeks to identify a pattern in the inputs before directing them to one of its Basis Functions, a localized transformation function appropriate to the pattern identified.

Development of ANN Methodology
Much of the work carried out in ANNs for forecasting has revolved less around the development of software and more around the configuration of the network, data management and performance measures.

Network Configuration
This task determines the architecture of the network, which includes such decisions as the number of layers used and the number of nodes in each layer. Additionally, the designer needs to select an activation function for the hidden and output layers and to set up the training algorithm (usually the back propagation algorithm) with an appropriate step size.

Network Architecture
The design of the network is usually problem dependent, there being no clear-cut 'formula' for determining the number of layers and nodes within each layer.

In selecting the number of input nodes, parsimony is a desirable feature, but not at the expense of leaving out variables with significant explanatory power. For time series forecasting problems, the number of lagged observations used to find patterns in the data would be one source of input nodes, but a designer could also incorporate other data such as that relating to economic conditions for financial market data. This would, potentially, enable the network to make one set of predictions in, for example, a low inflation scenario and another set in a higher inflation scenario, both based upon the same time series lagged variable pattern. The selection of input nodes will remain an art rather than a science, based partly on intuition and partly on empirical ideas, but always treading a tightrope between too few and too many inputs.

One of the main hazards of designing the hidden layer is that, if too many hidden nodes are used in an individual layer, the generalization ability of the network suffers. This is due to the network following the noise in the data, and as a result 'overfitting' of the function that the ANN is approximating. Research has shown that networks with two hidden layers perform better than those with one, but that there is no great improvement in performance with the addition of further layers.

The number of output nodes should be fairly apparent from the problem studied. For time-series forecasting, designers can construct either a one-step-ahead (ie for the next time period) or a multi-step-ahead network. Work has been carried out to make multi-step forecasts from one set of forecasts (by using the outputs as inputs to produce the next period's forecasts) and directly by configuring the ANN to have several output nodes to directly forecast each subsequent period into the future. There is currently no conclusive evidence that one approach is better than the other.

Activation Function

The activation function determines how inputs are directed from input nodes to hidden layers, between hidden nodes and from hidden nodes to outputs. It is possible for ANNs to have different activation functions for different nodes, but most networks have been designed to have the same activation function. As stated above, the most popular choice of network designers has been the sigmoid logistic function. Although it has been shown that feedforward ANNs with linear activation functions at the output node layer cannot cope adequately with time series data containing trends, more research into the relative benefits of linear and non-linear activation functions would be welcome.

Training Algorithm

The steps involved in ANN training are as follows:

- ▶ Deciding how many hidden nodes are to be used for each test network

- ▶ Setting up initial arc weights for each test network

- ▶ Partitioning data sets into:

▶ Training sets

▶ A validation set (to establish when training should stop)

▶ Test sets (to determine the performance of the network, in terms of forecasting ability)

The training of an ANN involves an iterative process of modifying arc weights to minimize the error between the target weight (as provided in the training data set) and the actual output value (as calculated by the network) for all of the training sets presented to it thus far.

The key to efficient training of an ANN lies in the selection of an appropriate step size, which determines the magnitude of the arc weight changes as new training sets are presented. Also important is the selection of initial weights, for which Tarassenko (1998) proposes that ten sets of initial weights should be used (ie ten different networks should be trained with different starting weights) for each network configuration considered.

The most common training method, the 'error back-propagation algorithm', used for updating the weights is highly sensitive to the learning rate selected. Importantly, it will not converge to the same set of optimal weights whatever learning rate is selected. Smaller learning rates tend to slow the learning process – the danger being that you run out of data sets before the optimal set of arc weights has been reached. Larger weights tend to cause excessive fluctuation or oscillation in weight changes. This problem has led to the proposal of an additional 'momentum' parameter, which is designed to facilitate faster convergence, whilst minimizing oscillation. However, there is no systematic method for choosing the learning rate and the momentum parameter, which are generally selected using experimentation.

Data Management

It has become clear through extensive research into ANNs that the availability of data in sufficient quantity and quality is absolutely crucial to the success of ANNs in forecasting.

While it is important for the ANN to be as parsimonious as possible, largely to avoid the previously mentioned hazard of overfitting, it is also vital that all relevant and possibly relevant data is considered at the outset of an ANN training programme. The highly desirable feature of ANNs is that the precise nature of the relationship between input and output variables does not need to be known; there only needs to be a strong possibility of a relationship (in the opinion of the network designer) for certain input variables to be included.

Tessarenko (1998) argues strongly that data should be stored in its raw form, ie without any pre-processing. Pre-processing, he argues, could remove important aspects of the data. The arc weights could, for example, be configured, to remove issues concerning scaling etc. Prior to use for training a neural network, the data needs to be validated by checking that it falls within an expected range. Any data falling outside this range needs to be examined, checked and either modified, or the expected range extended. In addition, all of the data to be used in an input 'vector', ie the group of inputs representing a discrete data set, needs to be checked for consistency, eg whether they all relate to the same time period.

Data management is another area where there is no clear formula for success; optimal results can only really be achieved through experience and experimentation.

Performance

Although the ultimate measure of an ANN is its predictive power, academic forecasters have proposed tests based on the differences between predicted output values and actual output values. These have included mean absolute deviation, sum of squared error, mean squared error (MSE) etc. Zhang et al (1998) propose that, in order to incorporate the risk of overfitting through having too many input parameters, the MSE is adjusted for degrees of freedom, which in turn is dependent upon the number of input parameters.

Extensive work has been carried out in comparing the predictive performance of ANNs with well established statistical models such as autoregressive moving average (ARMA) and autoregressive integrated moving average (ARIMA)[44] models. The results of this work have shown that ANNs generally perform better where relationships are more complex,

---

[44] Also known as the Box Jenkins model.

either being non-linear or being affected by seasonal trends. What is clear is that the relative results are dependent upon the periodicity selected (eg an ANN might outperform an ARMA model with weekly but not monthly data) and also upon the training of the ANN. Underperformance has also been found where relationships are linear with little noise. Additionally, research has shown that, where an ANN has underperformed and then re-trained, it can subsequently outperform traditional models.

Application Subject Areas

ANNs have been applied across a broad range of forecasting problems. These include financial forecasting of prices, including foreign exchange rates and commodity prices as well as electrical load, transportation and many other areas.

The clear message is that ANNs have a role to play in forecasting generally. In all but a few cases ANNs have provided superior forecasting for either all periodicities, or for a specific periodicity. It is also clear that the comparison of the performance of ANNs against traditional methods is a very useful one, particularly since ANNs are a 'black box' type of solution, and therefore not open to the same scrutiny as more traditional models.

Conclusion

There is a clear role for ANNs to play in forecasting, particularly where relationships between data are complex and hard to define. However, a great deal of preparatory work needs to be carried out, especially in preparing data for and training the ANN, which is more of an art than a science. It is also clear from the requirement correctly to specify the number of nodes, the learning rate and other key system parameters that the design and implementation of ANNs is a highly skilled and specialist task which also requires a good deal of experience. In order for ANNs to be accepted by, for example, practitioners in financial markets, a clear track record of predictive power needs to be established. The comparison of results with traditional forecasting methods provides a useful benchmark, as do performance metrics such as the adjusted MSE measure proposed by Zhang et al (1998).

Detailed Performance Calculations

1. Calculations Required
(a) Performance Returns

(i) Stock Level Returns

Daily time-weighted returns are to be used to calculate performance returns. For each day stock returns are to be calculated using the following formula:

$$R_N = \frac{V_E - V_B - C + I}{V_B}$$

where: R_N is the stock return for day N

V_E is the value of the stock at the end of day N

V_B is the value of the stock at the start of day N

C is purchases/sales of stock or

cash contributions/withdrawals into/out of fund

I is any income *accrued* to that stock on that day

Performance for each stock for the period is then calculated by chain-linking daily returns to produce a period return:

$$R_{(0-N)} = \{(1 + R_1) \times (1 + R_2) \times ... \times (1 + R_N)\} - 1$$

where: $R_{(0-N)}$ is the stock return from the end of day 0 to the end of day N

Returns can then be weighted by the proportion of the fund represented by that stock to give a weighted contribution of that stock to the fund's overall performance:

$$\text{contribution} = \sum_{n=0}^{N} w_n R_n$$

where: w = stock weight at the *start* of day n

(ii) Performance Analysis for Classification Levels

Stock level return contributions *cannot* simply be added to calculate returns above this level (eg industry, market, fund), they must be *separately* calculated at each level using the stock return and chain-linking calculations specified above.

A simple two stock fund example will bring out this point.

The return for the fund on the first day, where no transactions have taken place, can be calculated correctly from underlying weighted stock returns.

	Market Value Start Day 1	Market Value End Day 1	Net Acquisitions Day 1	Day 1 Return	Cumulative Return Day 1	Weight Start Day 1	Weighted Return	Cumulative Return from Weighted Stock Returns
Total Fund	10,000,000	10,200,000	0	2.0%	2.0%	100%		2.0%
Stock A	6,000,000	6,600,000	0	10.0%	10.0%	60%	6.0%	6.0%
Stock B	4,000,000	3,600,000	0	-10.0%	-10.0%	40%	-4.0%	-4.0%

However, if in day 2 there is a transaction, the cumulative returns can no longer be calculated correctly using this method, but must be calculated separately at each level.

	Market Value Start Day 1	Market Value End Day 1	Net Acquisitions Day 1	Day 1 Return	Cumulative Return Day 1	Weight Start Day 1	Weighted Return	Cumulative Return from Weighted Stock Returns
Total Fund	10,200,000	10,950,000	0	7.4%	9.5%	100%		10.5%
Stock A	6,600,000	3,150,000	-3,000,000	-6.8%	2.5%	65%	1.6%	7.7%
Stock B	3,600,000	7,800,000	3,000,000	-33.3%	-20.0%	35%	7.1%	2.8%

Otherwise a serious error is encountered (here 1%). This error will occur for any classification level above stock level, where a transaction has taken place.

(iii) Relative Returns

Benchmark returns are calculated in the same way as above.

Relative returns to be calculated as follows:

either: $\qquad R_R = \{(1 + R_F)/(1 + \overline{R_B})\} - 1$

or: $\qquad R_R = R_F - R_B$

(b) Performance Attribution

Attribution is to be calculated as follows.

(i) Currency Attribution

Currency Management

Currency Management $= \Sigma\{(wF_c - wB_c)(r_c - rB)\}$

where: $\quad wF_c \quad$ is the fund weight in currency C

$\qquad wB_c \quad$ is the benchmark weight in currency C

$\qquad r_c \qquad$ is the return from currency C calculated as the appreciation of spot rates relative to the forward rate in effect at the start of the measurement period

$$r_c = \frac{f_B - s_E}{s_E}$$

where: $\quad f_B =$ forward rate in effect at beginning

$\qquad s_E =$ spot rate in effect at end

$\qquad rB$ is the overall (ie weighted average using benchmark weights) return from currencies in the benchmark return

(ii) Market Attribution

Whereas market attribution for equities is calculated from percentage bets against the benchmark, for bonds it is calculated from weighted duration bets against the benchmark.

(a) Equities

Market Allocation $= \Sigma \{(wF_M - wB_M)(r_{CH}B_M - r_{CH}\overline{B})\}$

where: wF_M is the fund weight in market M

   wB_M is the benchmark weight in market M

   $r_{CH}B_M$ is the benchmark currency hedged return from market M

where: $r_{CH}\overline{B}$ is the overall (ie weighted average) benchmark currency hedged return from all markets:

$$r_{CH}\overline{B} = \Sigma(wB_M)(r_{CH}B_M)$$

(For calculation formulae for currency hedged returns, which account for the forward premiums or discounts effective during the period, please refer to the final section of this appendix).

(b) Bonds

The following calculation computes the fund return purely due to allocation across different bond markets:

$$\text{Market Allocation} = \sum_m^M \left\{ \left(\frac{w_m D_m F_m - w_m D_m B_m}{w_m D_m B_m} \right) (w_m B_m)(r_{CH}B_M - r_{CH}\overline{B}) \right\}$$

where: $w_m D_m F_m$ is the weighted duration for the fund in market m

   $w_m D_m B_m$ is the weighted duration for the benchmark in market m

   $w_m B_m$ is the benchmark weight in market m

   $r_{CH}B_m$ is the currency hedged return for each market in the benchmark

   $r_{CH}B$ is the weighted average currency hedged return for all markets in benchmark

(iii) Portfolio Duration Effect

Where a portfolio has a duration different to that of the benchmark, the impact of that duration position can be measured in relative terms using:

Portfolio Duration Effect =

$$= \sum_{m}^{M} \left\{ \left(\frac{w_m D_m F_m - w_m D_m B_m}{w_m D_m B_m} \right) \ (w_m B_m)(\overline{r_{CH} B} - r_{BC}) \right\}$$

Where: $\overline{r_{CH} B}$ is the weighted average currency hedged return for all markets in the benchmark

r_{BC} base currency interest return

NB This is not a subsequent hierarchical analysis level to market allocation, but should be considered as another view of the portfolio's performance.

(iv) Yield Curve Allocation

The following calculation computes the fund return due to yield curve allocation. Yield curve analysis should be decomposable into maturity bandings as required for each analysis:

Yield Curve Allocation =

$$= \sum_{m_y}^{M} \left\{ \left(\frac{w_{m_y} D_{m_y} F_{m_y} - w_{m_y} D_{m_y} B_{m_y}}{w_{m_y} D_{m_y} B_{m_y}} \right) \ (w_{m_y} B_{m_y})(\overline{r_{CH} B_M}) \right\}$$

where: $w_{m_y} D_{m_y} F_{m_y}$ is the weighted duration for the fund in the maturity band y within market m

$\overline{r_{CH} B_M}$ is the benchmark return in currency hedged terms for each market

(v) Stock Selection

Whereas stock selection for equities is calculated from relative returns for each market in the fund against that market's benchmark return, for bonds it is calculated by looking at the return on the fund in conjunction with the relative weighted duration of the fund compared with the benchmark.

(a) Equities

Stock Selection $= \Sigma\{(wF_M)(r_BF_M - r_BB_M)\}$

where: $\quad r_BF_M \quad$ is the fund's return from market M in base currency terms

$\quad r_BB_M \quad$ is the benchmark return from market M in base currency terms

More detailed stock selection is to be provided through analysis of the weighted performance of stocks within the classification level immediately above it (eg industry or market).

(b) Bonds

The following calculation gives the stock selection effect given the weighted duration invested. This is calculated from the outperformance of the fund and the benchmark relative to the base currency interest rate (ie the risk-free rate) and adjusting for duration.

$$\text{Stock Selection} = \sum_m^M \left\{ (r_{CH}F_m - r_{BC}) \left(\frac{r_{CH}B_m - r_{BC}}{w_mD_mB_m} \right) (w_mD_mF_m) \right\}$$

where: $\quad w_mD_mF_m \quad$ is the weighted duration for the fund in market m (giving the fund duration)

$\quad w_mD_mB_m \quad$ is the weighted duration for the benchmark in market m (giving the benchmark duration)

$\quad r_{BC} \quad$ is the base currency interest rate for each market

$\quad r_{CH}F_m \quad$ is the currency hedged return for the fund in each market

(vi) Residual

A small residual is expected due to intraday changes in asset allocation, benchmark anomalies etc. The sum of Currency Management, Market Allocation and Stock Selection should, however, be approximately equal to the fund's outperformance over the benchmark for the period.

2. Income

Income is to be treated as follows.

(a) Equities

Dividends are to be recognized for each stock on entitlement through the passing of a dated cash transaction related to that stock. The subsequent receipt of the dividend is then simply treated as an injection of cash into the Cash Sub-Portfolio dated the date of actual receipt into the fund.

The following example shows the correct treatment of the events from before ex-dividend date to the point where the cash is received.

Allocation of Market Values

	31/12/95	01/01/96	02/01/96	03/01/96	04/01/96
	Start	ICI Goes XD	BMW Up 10%	ICI Up 10%	ICI Dividend Paid
Total Fund	4000	4000	4300	4390	4390
UK Sub-Portfolio	1000	1000	1000	1090	990
ICI	1000	900	900	990	990
ICI Accrued Income	0	100	100	100	0
Europe Ex-UK Sub-Portfolio	3000	3000	3300	3300	3300
BMW	3000	3000	3300	3300	3300
Cash Sub-Portfolio	0	0	0	0	100

Performance

	01/01/96	02/01/96	03/01/96	04/01/96	Cumulative Period
	ICI Goes XD	*BMW Up 10%*	*ICI Up 10%*	*ICI Dividend Paid*	
Total Fund	0.00	7.50	2.09	0.00	9.75
UK Sub-Portfolio	0.00	0.00	9.00	0.00	9.00
ICI	0.00	0.00	10.00	0.00	10.00
Europe Ex-UK Sub-Portfolio	0.00	10.00	0.00	0.00	10.00
BMW	0.00	10.00	0.00	0.00	10.00
Cash Sub-Portfolio	0.00	0.00	0.00	0.00	0.00

The implication of the above is that when the dividend is actually received, it will have to tell the system to remove the accrued element of the return from the stock from that day onward. A complication here may be that the actual amount received will normally differ (less usually) from the amount accrued; thus a simple cancelling out will not be possible.

Where income is received as a scrip dividend, the same principle should apply, with an accrual of the value of the stock marked to market on that date. The receipt of the dividend should be treated as an injection of stock into the relevant sub-portfolio, valued using the market value for that stock at that point in time.

(b) Fixed Interest

For performance purposes, dirty, cum-dividend pricing is to be used.

With regard to performance analysis, industry best practice is different for bonds and equities. Whereas it is best practice to accrue interest on equities on XD date, this approach would lead to a distortion of the performance of fixed interest securities since the net present value of the coupon payment would not be taken into account. Diagrammatically we want to present prices to the system for performance calculations as follows (following the solid line).

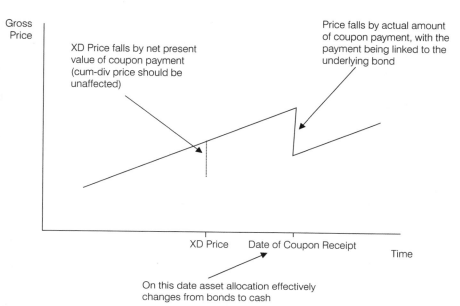

For example:

A bond currently priced at 100 with a coupon payment of 10 due in 30 days from now goes XD.

Interest rates are 6%.

The price will fall by the net present value of the coupon payment, calculated as follows:

$$10 \times \left(1 - \left(\frac{30}{360} \times 0.06\right)\right) = 9.95$$

Thus we cannot use the full coupon to compensate for the fall in price, since this will overestimate the true value of the bond.

The main points that we need to be certain about when pricing bonds within the performance system are:

(1) That on XD date, and for the period between XD date and the date of coupon receipt, the cum-div price is calculated correctly, ie incorporating the net present value as I have described above.

(2) That on the date of the receipt of the coupon, the price falls by the full amount of the coupon receipt and that the receipt is linked (through the associated SEDOL) to the bond.

It is *essential*, therefore, that a coupon receipt transaction is generated for fixed-interest securities.

c) *Cash*
Interest on cash balances held is to be accrued on a daily basis and included in returns for the appropriate sub-portfolio.

3. Injections and Withdrawals

(a) *Cash*
Where new money is injected into a fund, or cash is withdrawn to meet a liability, it should be paid into/withdrawn from the Cash Sub-Portfolio.

(b) *Stock*
Normally as a result of funds being merged, or movements between fund managers, there are injections/(withdrawals) in the form of increases/decreases to stock positions.

The utopian requirement is for stock transfers to be transacted using the market price of the security at the time of the transaction. This needs to be captured at deal entry time, perhaps with reference to Reuters, to give the true value at that time.

An acceptable interim solution would be to use the closing market price of the security for the day of the transfer.

4. Cash Allocations

(a) *Sub-Portfolio Cash*
Specifically looking towards future requirements for AIMR compliance, the system should be configured to facilitate cash allocations to particular sub-portfolios. These sub-portfolios correspond to particular desks, eg UK, US, Japan, Europe, FICG etc.

This will allow 'carve-outs' to be created, with their own allocated cash. As in 2(c) above, interest on this cash should be accrued daily.

(b) Cash Backing Futures

Where a sub-portfolio holds a future, an amount of cash backing equivalent to the effective exposure of the future should be allocated to that sub-portfolio. For performance purposes, this should be treated as a positive amount of cash accruing interest on a daily basis. If a future is shorted, the corresponding cash backing figure will be negative. It should also be combined with the performance of the future itself (this combination being a 'futures strategy') to give a return comprising of both the return from the future and the interest earned on the cash backing.

5. Performance Analysis of Models

In general, the performance analysis of models is to be carried out through the use of model funds which represent the positions taken by the fund manager at different levels, as well as benchmark positions.

Performance will be calculated at each classification level through:

$$R_{MODEL} = \{(\text{Model Position}) - (\text{Benchmark Position})\} \times \text{Return on Asset Class}$$

This approach will also facilitate risk and hedging analysis (eg what would the performance have been without the hedging strategy).

Enough flexibility should be available to enable analysis to be carried out in the same way that decisions were taken. For example, if decisions were made to gain exposure to certain industries (or groups of industries such as cyclicals, defensives, interest rate sensitive etc), irrespective of market, performance analysis should be available to support this.

Performance analysis of currencies is to be carried out as follows (relative to base currency):

$$\text{Local Currency Return} = E_c \times \frac{S_0}{S_1}$$

$$\text{Base Currency Return} = (E_c \times (1 + r_{CH})(1 + r_L) - 1) + (H_c \times \frac{S_1}{_0 f_1}) - 1$$

where: E_c = Exposure to currency C through security investment

r_{CH} = Currency hedged return

r_L = Local currency return

H_C = Currency hedge (expressed as a percentage) out of currency C

s_0 = Spot exchange rate at time 0 from currency C to base

s_1 = Spot exchange rate at time 1 from currency C to base

$_0f_1$ = Forward exchange rate at time 0 for time 1 from currency C to base

Multi-Period Model Analysis

Returns should be calculated separately for each sub-period for which a decision was effective. These should then be chain-linked to provide analysis for the overall period.

6. Pricing

The pricing source used for both securities held and index constituents (ie those not held in client funds) must be consistent. Where a single source cannot supply the prices for the entire universe of securities, stocks not priced from this source should be priced from OPUS.

7. Risk Analysis

Having calculated performance returns as above, the system should also be able provide risk analysis calculated as the standard deviation of returns. Additionally, tracking error (standard deviation of relative returns) should also be fairly easy to produce.

Five years' worth of returns should be the target to provide the ultimate level of reporting. A minimum of two years' worth of returns is required to provide any meaningful analysis.

8. Transaction History Required

Obviously the greater the period for which reliable transaction data is available, the better, especially for analysis of risk.

It would be feasible to run the system starting without any history. Two years' worth of transaction data would give an acceptable level of reporting.

9. Currency Hedged Returns

Currency hedged returns account for the forward premiums or discounts in effect for the period of measurement. Forward premiums are based on interest rate differentials between the local currency and the fund's base currency and are related to forward currency rates (under the Interest Rate Parity theory) as follows.

$$\frac{X_{F_{B.L}}}{X_{S_{B.L}}} = \frac{(1 + R_L)}{(1 + R_B)}$$

where: $X_{F_{B.L}}$ is the forward rate for the period between base and local currency

$X_{S_{B.L}}$ is the current spot rate between base and local currency

R_L is the interest rate return on local cash for the period

R_B is the interest rate return on base currency cash for the period

For example, if interest rates in Japanese yen are 0.5%, and in sterling (fund's base currency) are 6%, and the spot exchange rate is 1 yen = £0.006, the theory states that the forward rate can be found by:

$$\frac{X_{F_{B.L}}}{0.006} = \frac{1.005}{1.06}$$

$$\therefore X_{F_{B.L}} = 0.0057$$

Currency hedged returns can be approximated using the following calculation, which would be a good starting point for this type of calculation:

$$\left(\frac{(S_E \times MV_{E_L}) + ((_B f_E \times MV_{B_L}) - (S_E \times MV_{BL}))}{(S_B \times MV_{B_L})} \right) -1$$

where: S_E is the base to local spot rate at the end of the period (eg for a yen-based investor 1Y = £0.006)

MV_{EL} is the market value in local terms at the end of the period

MV_{BL} is the market value in local terms at the beginning of the period

r_L is the local cash return for the period

r_B is the base currency cash return for the period

$$_B f_E = \left(\frac{90}{91} \, S_0 + \frac{1}{91} \, _0 f_{91} \right)$$ to give the currency hedged return in day 1, irrespective of whether the currency is hedged in day 2

However, to provide a truly utopian currency hedged return, changes in forward premiums (driven by changes in interest rate differentials between the fund base currency and local currency), and changes in market value resulting in the currency being over- or underhedged should be accounted for on a daily basis, with the resulting returns chain-linked. To calculate the currency hedged return for Day 1, the following formula is to be used (using a strategy based on one month rolling forwards):

$$\left[\frac{MV_{0_L} \, \dfrac{S_1}{S_1 - OP_{30} + P_{31}}}{MV_{0_L S_0}} \right] + \left[\left(\frac{(MV_{1_L} - MV_{0_L})}{MV_{0_L}} \right) \left(\frac{S_0}{S_1} \right) \right]$$

where: $_0 P_1$ is the forward premium effective for the period from 0 to 30 days

$$r_{CH_{(0,8)}} = [(1 + r_{CH_{(0,1)}}) \times \ldots \times (1 + r_{CH_{(R-1,n)}})] - 1$$

The currency hedged return for the period from 0 through to n days is then simply calculated as follows.

Performance Analysis of Forward Currency Deals

In order to provide a performance system for the analysis of foreign currency deals which is comprehensive and flexible, the system requires the following transaction data.

For the initial trade

1. Currency Sold to Fund Base Currency

2. To balance (1) corresponding equal and opposite transaction from Fund Base to Currency Sold, referenced back to the security identifier for (1)

3. Currency Bought to Fund Base Currency

4. To balance (3) corresponding equal and opposite transaction from Currency Bought to Fund Base, referenced back to the security identifier for (3)

Upon maturity of the trade Converting Forward to Spot Cash

5–8. Equal and opposite of deals in 1–4 above to represent the conversion of the forward to a spot two days prior to maturity

9–12. Spot trades as per 1–4 above

Example transactions used attached.

Return Calculation

Where an asset or class is not held throughout the entire period of measurement the return for that asset or class should be flagged as 'N/A'. Returns should, however, be calculated for the class or fund to which the asset or class belongs. If a fund itself is not in existence for the entire period, the return should also be flagged as 'N/A'.

Where there is a negative market value at the start of the period, the performance return for that asset, class (or fund) should be flagged as 'N/A'.

Transaction Level Analysis

Fund G010Z12	18/01/96 Start MV	18/01/96 End MV	Income	Net Acquisitions	Return	Cumulative Return
Fund Total	−12079.29	−9830.32	0	0	−0.186183644	−0.186183644
FWD FIM 19/1/96 TEST	7342.04	7349.81	0	0	0.001058372	0.001058372
FWD £ 19/1/96 TEST	−411450.07	−411450.07	0	0	0	0
FWD $ 19/1/96 TEST	392028.75	394269.94	0	0	0.005716914	0.005716914
SPOT FIM 21/6/96 TEST	0	0	0	0	N/A	N/A
SPOT GBP 21/01/96 TEST	0	0	0	0	N/A	N/A
SPOT USD 21/6/96 TEST	0	0	0	0	N/A	N/A

Fund G010Z12	19/01/96 Start MV	19/01/96 End MV	Income	Net Acquisitions	Return	Cumulative Return
Fund Total	−9830.32	−6858.15	0	0	−0.30234724	−0.432238773
FWD FIM 19/1/96 TEST	7349.81	0	−7372.46	0	0.003081687	0.004143321
FWD £ 19/1/96 TEST	−411450.07	0	309643.2	0	−0.24743439	−0.24743439
FWD $ 19/1/96 TEST	394269.94	0	−302271	0	−0.233340706	−0.22895778
SPOT FIM 21/6/96 TEST	0	7372.46	7372.46	0	N/A	N/A
SPOT GBP 21/01/96 TEST	0	−411450.07	−309643	0	N/A	N/A
SPOT USD 21/6/96 TEST	0	397219.46	302270.7	0	N/A	N/A

Fund G010Z12	22/01/96 Start MV	22/01/96 End MV	Income	Net Acquisitions	Return	Cumulative Return
Fund Total	−6858.15	−8089.63	0	0	0.179564819	−0.330288831
FWD FIM 19/1/96 TEST	0	0	0	0	N/A	N/A
FWD £ 19/1/96 TEST	0	0	0	0	N/A	N/A
FWD $ 19/1/96 TEST	0	0	0	0	N/A	N/A
SPOT FIM 21/6/96 TEST	7372.46	7294.69	0	0	−0.010548123	N/A
SPOT GBP 21/01/96 TEST	−411450.07	−411450.07	0	0	0	N/A
SPOT USD 21/6/96 TEST	397219.46	396065.75	0	0	−0.002904482	N/A

Fund G010Z12	23/01/96 Start MV	23/01/96 End MV	Income	Net Acquisitions	Return	Cumulative Return
Fund Total	−8089.63	−7871.5	0	0	−0.026964868	−0.348347505
FWD FIM 19/1/96 TEST	0	0	0	0	N/A	N/A
FWD £ 19/1/96 TEST	0	0	0	0	N/A	N/A
FWD $ 19/1/96 TEST	0	0	0	0	N/A	N/A
SPOT FIM 21/6/96 TEST	7294.69	7277.38	0	0	−0.002372427	N/A
SPOT GBP 21/01/96 TEST	−411450.07	−411450.07	0	0	0	N/A
SPOT USD 21/6/96 TEST	396065.75	396301.19	0	0	0.000594452	N/A

Transactions Used

"G010Z12", "SELLCCY", "FWDGBP", 411450.07000,1.0000000, "GBP", 0,
"GBP", 0, "GBP", 411450.07000, "GBP", 960117,960119, "NMR","", "86797S",
,,"","","","","C"

"G010Z12", "BUYBASE", "FWDFIM", 2100000.0000,1.0000000,"FIM",
0,"FIM", 0,"FIM", 2100000.0000,"FIM", 960117,960119,"NMR ","FWDGBP",
"86797SC",,,"","","","","C"

"G010Z12", "BUYCCY", "FWDUSD", 600000.000000,1.0000000,"USD",
0,"USD", 0,"USD", 600000.00000,"USD", 960117,960119,"NMR ","",
"86797B",,,"","","","","C"

"G010Z12", "SELBASE", "FWDFIM", 2050000.0000,1.0000000,"FIM", 0,"FIM",
0,"FIM", 2050000.0000,"FIM", 960117,960119,"NMR ","FWDUSD",
"86797BC",,,"","","","","C"

"G010Z12", "FWD-MAT", "FWDGBP", 411450.07000,1.0000000,"GBP",
0,"GBP", 0,"GBP", 411450.07000,"GBP", 960119,960119,"NMR ","",
"86798S",,,"","","","","C"

"G010Z12", "BSE+MAT", "FWDFIM", 2100000.0000,1.0000000,"FIM",
0,"FIM", 0,"FIM", 2100000.0000,"FIM", 960119,960119,"NMR ","FWDGBP",
"86798SC",,,"","","","","C"

"G010Z12", "FWD+MAT", "FWDUSD", 600000.00000,1.0000000,"USD",
0,"USD", 0,"USD", 600000.00000,"USD", 960119,960119,"NMR ","",
"86798B",,,"","","","","C"

"G010Z12", "BSE-MAT", "FWDFIM", 2050000.0000,1.0000000,"FIM", 0,"FIM",
0,"FIM", 2050000.0000,"FIM", 960119,960119,"NMR ","FWDUSD",
"86798BC",,,"","","","","C"

"G010Z12", "SELLCCY", "SPOTGBP", 411450.07000,1.0000000,"GBP",
0,"GBP", 0,"GBP", 411450.07000,"GBP", 960119,960121,"NMR ","",
"86798S",,,"","","","","C"

225

```
"G010Z12", "BUYBASE", "SPOTFIM", 2100000.0000,1.0000000,"FIM",
0,"FIM", 0,"FIM", 2100000.0000,"FIM", 960119,960121,"NMR ","SPOTGBP",
"86798SC", ,,"", "" , ,, "" , , ", "C"

"G010Z12", "BUYCCY", "SPOTUSD", 600000.00000,1.0000000,"USD",
0,"USD", 0,"USD", 600000.00000,"USD", 960119,960121,"NMR ","",
"86798B", ,,"", "" , ,, "" , , ", "C"

"G010Z12", "SELBASE", "SPOTFIM", 2050000.0000,1.0000000,"FIM",
0,"FIM", 0,"FIM", 2050000.0000,"FIM", 960119,960121,"NMR ","SPOTUSD",
"86798BC", ,,"", "" , ,, "" , , ", "C"
```

APPENDIX X

Average Book Cost Calculation

Book cost is generally calculated as an average, since a stock may have been purchased in a number of tranches.

Marks and Spencer (Current Position)		320,000	
Transaction Date	Transaction Type	Quantity	Price Dealt
20/04/2001	BUY	400,000	2.02
05/05/2001	BUY	240,000	2.06
18/05/2001	SELL	500,000	2.20
20/05/2001	BUY	180,000	2.10

The book cost of this position would be calculated in the UK on a 'First In First Out (FIFO)' basis. Thus the two initial trades would have an average book price of:

$$\text{Book Price} = \frac{(400,000 \times 2.02) + (240,000 \times 2.06)}{640,000} = 2.035$$

The assumption would be that 500,000 stocks with a book price of 2.035 were sold on 18/05/2001, leaving 140,000 stocks with a book cost of £284,900. The transaction on the 20th May would change the book price to:

$$\text{Book Price} = \frac{(140,000 \times 2.035) + (180,000 \times 2.10)}{320,000} = 2.035$$

Giving a book cost for the position of £662,900.

The Myners Report

This appendix provides a very high level overview of the issues raised by the Report. It is well worth reading the Report in full.

Introduction

Further to a study of US market practice, the UK's Labour Government came to believe that economic growth could be enhanced through the regeneration of the UK manufacturing sector. This, they considered, should take the form of private sector funding of small to medium size businesses to enable them to take advantage of the technological revolution. The availability of private equity or venture capital funding is, however, extremely thin on the ground. Particularly in pension fund investment, it was found that fund management companies 'herded' around large company investment (typically those featuring as quoted constituents of the major indices, such as the FTSE 100 and MSCI World indices).

The dearth of investment in smaller companies contradicts the principles of modern portfolio theory (eg the Capital Asset Pricing Model, which is based on the premise that all investors should hold portfolios consisting of *all* available assets). The strong implication is that capital is being inefficiently allocated within the UK economy. The Myners Report was commissioned to investigate this phenomenon and to make recommendations that would reverse this trend.

Paul Myners is the Chairman of Gartmore Investment Management, one of the most respected names in the industry.

Findings

General

It is probably safe to say that the Myners Report reached further into the issues facing professional investors than was strictly required by its remit. The resulting document proposes nothing short of a revolution across the investment management board, and within the pension fund management industry in particular.

Inefficient Capital Allocation

The Myners Report identified the following barriers to the efficient allocation of capital across the economy. In addition, the issues discussed were felt to hinder the fund manager in his objective of meeting the pension (or other liability) obligation of the fund.

Asset Allocation

The weight of academic evidence supports the assertion that most of a portfolio's performance emanates from asset allocation (ie allocation between markets). The Myners Report finds that, in its opinion, insufficient resources are assigned to this function.

Setting Peer Group Benchmarks

Most pension funds have peer group benchmarks, ie an implied 'neutral' weighting equal to the average allocation of capital by all pension fund managers. The impact of this is the encouragement to 'herd' around the same (large capitalization) securities, rather than looking at the objectives of the fund and making an independent choice.

Timescales

Fund managers were found to have vague performance timescales (ie over what time period their performance would be measured). This leads to a short-termist investment approach, again leading to investment in a narrower group of securities.

Minimum Funding Requirement (MFR)

The MFR, which was introduced in the early 1990s, was an attempt to *ensure* that fund managers met their pension fund obligations. The Report found that the measure resulted in excessive fixed interest instrument investment, whatever the age or projected liability stream of the fund.

Broker Commissions

The Report considered that the payment of broking commission required greater scrutiny. The huge volume of commissions paid, justified by the provision of broker's research (which many commentators view as being largely superfluous), is a major cost to pension fund members.

Recommendations

The thrust of the Report's recommendation is towards a refocusing on the objectives of the fund, namely to be able to meet its liability stream obligations at a time in the future. In order to achieve this, the following recommendations were made:

- ▶ Training for the fund's trustees, in order that they can better challenge advice offered on the allocation of a fund's capital

- ▶ Review all pension benchmarks, explicitly considering their suitability given the ultimate objective of meeting the fund's liabilities

- ▶ Provide clear guidelines for fund managers with regard to the timescales to be used in measuring performance

- ▶ Replace the Minimum Funding Requirement with a transparent fund reporting requirement, where fund managers are required to clearly state their current asset allocation, and how they feel that their strategy will ensure that fund liability requirements are met.

In addition, and perhaps most controversially of all, the Myners Report recommended that brokers' commissions be rolled into fees charged to pension fund members (rather than being separately charged to clients as it is currently). The objective of this measure is to incentivize fund managers to consider whether they are getting value for money from the service provided by brokers.

This recommendation was far from well received in the City generally, since its adoption would inevitably greatly reduce the volume of broking commissions generated.

Glossary

AIMR	Association for Investment Management and Research (US body)
Broker	Intermediary obtaining securities in each market for the fund manager
Cable	Sterling/Dollar exchange rate
Cash Backing	Term used for a notional cash amount required to balance the actual exposure to a market gained through opening a futures position
Convexity	Measures the rate of change of bond prices with respect to interest rate. A second order term is required to explain differences in price changes predicted by rate changes using modified duration.
Custodian	Independent bank appointed to look after the client's physical assets (eg share certificates, bank accounts etc)
Freddie Mac	Securitized fixed-interest security. Underlying collateral is property in the *Federal Home Loan Mortgage Association*.
Ginnie Mae	Similar to Freddie Mac, but collateral is property in the *General Home Loan Mortgage Association*.
Fund of Funds	A holding fund which invests in units of other funds which themselves invest in securities
Hard Landing	Period of recession following an economic boom
IPO	Initial Public Offering. Shares offered to the investing public, subject to a set of rules, as a result of a corporate equity restructuring
January Effect	An empirically observed phenomenon whereby share prices trade higher at the start of the year

Liquidity

Availability of counterparties to trade with in a given security. If stock is illiquid, it generally commands a premium market price

Maturity Bucket

The grouping of fixed interest securities using ranges of years from now until maturity (eg all bonds in a portfolio/benchmark maturing between 10 and 15 years from now)

Margin

Cash payment required by futures exchanges to meet potential losses on a fund manager's position

PPP

Purchasing Power Parity – the theory stating that all equivalent goods should cost the same amount in some base currency. This implies, for example, that higher domestic inflation will cause a currency to depreciate over time

Risk Free Asset

An investment which is riskless, ie in terms of inflation risk, interest rate risk and default risk. An example might be a three month US Treasury Bill

Segregated Fund

A fund which invests across asset categories on behalf of one client (as contrasted with a unitized vehicle which anyone can invest in)

Settlement Cycle

The period between a market trade and the exchange of cash for securities

Trustees

An independent body, usually a bank independent of the asset manager, appointed to ensure that the asset manager is managing the fund according to the requirements of the client, as specified in the fund mandate

Index

A

Notes

Notes

Notes

Notes

Notes

Notes

Notes

Notes